Keewaydinoquay, Stories from My Youth

Keewaydinoquay,
Stories from My Youth

KEEWAYDINOQUAY PESCHEL

Edited by Lee Boisvert

The University of Michigan Press
Ann Arbor

Published in the United States of America by
The University of Michigan Press
Manufactured in the United States of America
♾ Printed on acid-free paper

2009   2008   2007   2006   4   3   2   1

A CIP catalog record for this book is available from the British Library.

Library of Congress Cataloging-in-Publication Data

Keewaydinoquay.
    Keewaydinoquay, stories from my youth / Keewaydinoquay
Peschel; edited by Lee Boisvert.
        p.   cm.
    ISBN-13: 978-0-472-09920-7 (cloth : alk. paper)
    ISBN-10: 0-472-09920-5 (cloth : alk. paper)
    ISBN-13: 978-0-472-06920-0 (pbk. : alk. paper)
    ISBN-10: 0-472-06920-9 (pbk. : alk. paper)
    1. Keewaydinoquay.   2. Ojibwa women—Biography.
3. Ojibwa philosophy. 4. Ojibwa Indians—Social life and customs.
I. Title: Stories from my youth.   II. Boisvert, Lee.   III. Title.

E99.C6K425   2006
977.004'97333—dc22   2005024417

Text design by Mary H. Sexton

Typesetting by Delmastype, Ann Arbor, Michigan

Text Font: Monotype Garamond
Monotype Garamond is based on roman types cut by Jean
Jannon in 1615, following the designs of Claude Garamond
that had been cut in the previous century. It is a beautiful
typeface with an air of informality that works well for
setting text.
                    —courtesy fonts.com

Display font: Journal Text
Journal was designed in 1990, as a digital font, by Zuzanna
Licko, co-founder of Emigre. Rather than resurrecting a
particular typeface from letterpress specimens, Journal is a
revival of the letterpress look itself. The irregularities that
appear in letterpress printing are simulated, which yields a
subtle crudeness that is apparent in laserwriter printouts as
well as high resolution typesetting.
                    —courtesy emigre.com

This book is dedicated to the Language Teachers,
who struggle to save all Native Language, but especially
to those who taught me: Don Able, Helen and George Roy,
Kenny Pheasant, Rosella Pheasant Kinoshameg,
Barbara Nolan, and Ray Kiogoma.

K'Chi Miigwech, Kinomaageniniwok
miinwaa Kinomaagenini Kwek
(Many thanks to the Teachers).

LEE BOISVERT
*Project Director for the Holy Hill Center, Incorporated
of Leland, Michigan*

Preface

The stories of our lives come from many places . . . memory, hopes and dreams, loss and fear, visions . . . teachings from times and experiences uncountable.

These stories of a young girl were told to us by an old woman, who lived through perhaps the most dramatic changes that our nation has seen. She grew up with canoe and horse and buggy and ended up flying around the world.

Keewaydinoquay is the author of this book. Kee spoke these words; she wrote them; she sang them and danced them and drew them and prayed them. The work of the committee has been but the collecting, minor editing, and arranging of her works.

Please take these stories as they are intended . . . to teach and entertain and enlighten and enrich the lives of those who wish to read them.

The Holy Hill Center, Incorporated

Books Written by Keewaydinoquay

These books are available in softcover from MKD Publications, P.O. Box 49, Kewadin, MI 49648.

The Girl Who Was Stolen by Owls
Dear Grandfathers
Our Grandmother Who Is Moon
Maumee and RedFeather
Brave Is Mahng Is Loon
Direction We Know: Walk in Honor
Sisters of the Moon Shields
The Old Man in the Stone Canoe
Mukwah Mishkomin or Kinnickinnick "Gift of Bear"
Min: Anishinaabeg Ogimaawi-minan BlueBerry: First Fruit of
     The People
Shingabiss

This book is available in hardcover from Educational Studies Press.

Puhpohwe for The People

Acknowledgments

This work would not have been possible without many months living with Keewaydinoquay while recording and transcribing stories, which often involved unending nightlong sessions with Grandmother. Two women in particular did the builk of this labor of love. Mitchi Miigwech to Anungoday Marcella Wanta Voyt and Barbara Leigh for their unstinting gifts of time and caring.

This project was supported by a grant from the Michigan Humanities Council, which is funded in part by the National Endowment for the Humanities.

We offer much gratitude to Mary Erwin, Christina Milton, and all the staff at the University of Michigan Press for their thoughtful and considerate relationship with this work and with us.

Also instrumental were Fay Stone, who got this project started after Keewaydinoquay walked on in 1999, and the members of the Holy Hill Center's Life Story Committee, whose efforts over the last three years were aimed at ensuring that this work was done as well as we humans can do it: Fay Stone as copy editor, and Barbara Leigh and Stanette Amy, who also provided editorial and creative input. Lee Boisvert was the project director and made all final decisions.

We also thank the members of our ad hoc advisory council, who accepted our humble petitions for their input: Jack Chambers, Linda Chambers, Terry Bussey, Jill Bedard and Alyssa Anthony.

We would like to thank our families and friends for their patience and support during the three years required for this work. Tahnahga Yako Myers kindly offered years of creative and cultural support, and Kathleen Bowman helped in many ways.

Many people were asked for advice and to read or to listen to various portions as the years went by: Bob and Adam Boisvert,

Linda Chambers, Janie Panagopolous, Judy Meister, Carol Larson, and Kathleen Misak. Miigwech to Frank Ettawageshik and John St. Augustine for their helpful input. We also thank the people of the Miniss Kitigan Drum for all that they do.

It is amazing what a community project this turned out to be. We could not have done it without the support of Laura Quackenbush of the Leelanau Historical Museum, Brian Price of the Leelanau Conservancy, Michelle of Horizon Books, Lori Wegner of Leelanau Books, the fourth-grade students of Dennis Snarey and Jennifer Hewlitt at the East Jordan public schools, and Maureen McCormick's high school students at the Forest Area schools.

Three businesses provided expert advice and service over the years: Copies Plus of Elk Rapids, Copy Central of Traverse City, and the Photo Center in Walgreen's Drugstore, also in Traverse City.

We appreciate the day spent with Keewaydinoquay's old high school teacher Mr. Cliff Ellinger and the many kindnesses offered by his friends Dorothy Holderbaum and John and Eleanor Nihikian. I thank Rita Bober for helping me get to Allegan.

Three people have contributed stories as they remember Keewaydinoquay telling them: Rich Maples, Stanette Amy, and Lee Boisvert.

The photo of the ice cave was taken by Rob Milton. Other photographs were taken by Lee Boisvert. The artwork is by Keewaydinoquay, except for the floral designs, which represent traditional Anishinaabeg beadwork patterns. The beadwork on the front cover was created by Lynnora Walczak.

Michigan**Humanities**Council
Bridging Communities and Ideas

Contents

Introduction

Welcome to a brief glimpse of just one human being. What is offered here represents only a small part of who and what Keewaydinoquay Margaret Peschel was. Our goal is simply to share with others the stories that our Nokomis (Grandmother) Keewaydinoquay shared with us.

The decades in which these stories are set were ones of great turmoil and change for Native people. In order to survive, literally, many families and individuals were forced to make the choice to be as "non-Indian" as possible. Decisions such as these continued to affect the generations that followed. The rights for Native Americans to work, live, and practice spiritual beliefs were rigidly controlled by the American government. It was not until 1978 that the American Indian Religious Freedom Act was signed into law. Now that many Native people have begun the laborious process of researching and reclaiming scattered heritage, there is even greater hunger to learn and preserve ancient knowledge.

Keewaydinoquay Margaret Peschel, born in 1918, is the only person of her time who we know studied both traditional Ojibway and Western medicines. As a young girl she studied with Native herbalists. She graduated from high school at the age of 17 in 1935. In 1944 she was granted a bachelor of science by Central Michigan University. In 1953 she was awarded a master of science with an emphasis in education in counseling and guidance. Her thesis for this degree was titled "The Science Excursion as a Guidance Technique." In 1977 she was awarded a master of science at Central Michigan University in Mt. Pleasant. Her thesis was titled "Reliving Algonkian Ethnobotany." From 1976 to 1978 she studied at the University of Michigan in Ann Arbor as a Ph.D. candidate in ethnobotany. These facts we do know, but many others have been lost in the mists of time and memory and perception.

From looking over the papers we do have, it is clear that Keewaydinoquay took classes and courses and workshops and asked a million questions from everyone she met throughout her lifetime. Keewaydinoquay loved learning, and the "bump of curiosity" she seemed to have been born with sent her far and wide. She was able to share this love with students from all over the globe. She appears to have come by this all very naturally. Her parents had met and were married in the Thumb area of Michigan but managed, between the two of them, to have more experiences than many of their generation, thanks in part to her father's service in the United States Marine Corps and to the colleges that both her parents attended.

The teachings of Keewaydinoquay, both written and oral, have contributed to the knowledge, and love, of plants for many people. They are read by scholars and children and families throughout the world.

Her formal teaching career in public schools began as a teenager and spanned more than three decades. In the last twenty years of her life, she taught in the Native American Studies Program at the University of Wisconsin–Milwaukee and also shared her knowledge at numerous workshops and in summer-long woodland encampments.

In addition to her skills as an ethnobotanist, with special knowledge of mycology, Keewaydinoquay was also a wife, mother, grandmother, writer, poet, rock hound, student, teacher, artist, and musician, as well as an extremely gifted storyteller. Perhaps the most important part of her life, though, was sharing the understanding that in all healthy relationships reciprocity is involved. This includes the relationship between humans and the plant kingdoms, as well as all others.

You will find that the spelling of Native words vary. This is because Anishinaabemowin (the language of the Anishinaabeg) was until recently primarily an oral language. How language is used also may be different than some have experienced before. Language usage changes over time, as does how language is expressed.

Everything written here took place before 1945 . . . before television and rocket ships . . . even before many people in rural areas had electricity in their homes.

This book is our attempt to take Kee's manuscripts—some edited by her and some not—plus her journals and papers for college classes, and combine them with the stories and teachings that she passed on to us orally. She tried valiantly to complete this project in her lifetime, and we wish she had been able to do so.

We have inserted material to help explain or clarify the texts. Brackets [ ] enclose the words we have added. We have tried to keep this to a minimum and hope they help. Material in parentheses ( ) was inserted by Keewaydinoquay herself, mostly in the texts she wrote.

The symbol ✳ separates the elements in some of the stories. It represents some of the symbols for stars that are used by many Native nations living on Turtle Island (America).

Many specific facts about Keewaydinoquay's life we do not know. What we can be sure of are these stories . . . full of excitement and wonder and a sense of timelessness that spans cultures and generations.

Many of the elders from these Before-Times are gone now. Too many of them have left us with their stories untold or unremembered. So let us treasure what, through the foresight and persistence of Keewaydinoquay, is shared here. Let these stories speak to us all . . . of the love of family and friends and Blessed Spirits uncountable . . . the true wealth and magic of Anishinaabeg People.

Blessings and Balance
Balance and Blessings
For from Balance
Comes All Blessings

Ahau!

The Circle of Trustees for the Holy Hill Center, Incorporated
of Leland, Michigan

Prologue

My life has been a continuous battle for the survival of self and honor. I can't remember myself without having been conscious of moral responsibilities . . . that it wasn't fair, but that's all. My grandfathers lived that way.

I feel I've been bombarded with difficult moral choices, but that could be because I've been conditioned for it.

I used to sorrow over all of it. I don't any more. I've lived long enough to know that practically everything we consider bad luck . . . sorrow, undeserved terror . . . contributes to the whole.

There are certain people, heroes, I want to include in these stories. They gave me such wonderful gifts, and I didn't realize it then. I never had a chance to thank them the way I wanted to. This has been on my mind ever since I went to Pearse's cabin and couldn't find him . . . .

Sometimes I wonder if your personality gets bent so you draw to yourself things of a certain nature . . . .

Earliest Memories

Stories of My Beginnings

Although my father was a college graduate, the Indian set of mind was never "educated out" of his personality, and if the [following] incident on the beach contained [an] echo of that condition, there was good reason. I had been the only natural child of Wauboshtigwan (Waub-osh-tig-wan) and Minosoahnikwe (Min-o-so-ah-ni-kwe) to survive this cycle.

During those days, there was no hospital in all of Leelanau County [Michigan]. The best Indian doctors were out on the islands. Everyone, white and Indian alike, was born at home, except for children of the very wealthy. Their womenfolk [the wealthy ones] traveled, a week before actual confinement, to medical facilities in some southern county, where, if one should judge by the results at that time, medical prestige was greater than medical facility. At the season of my approaching birth, my mother was approximately fifty. Well-meaning European friends persuaded my parents that their only hope for a living and mentally alert child was a hospital delivery. [In spite of trying for years, none of their earlier pregnancies had been able to produce a living baby.]

They had two horses but no sturdy passenger wagon. None of the "Nishnobs" had cars as yet.[1] But everyone had boats. The nearby (thirty-five miles away) owner of a good fishing boat

1. Nishnob is slang for Anishinaabeg–the People of the Three Fires (Ojibwa, Odawa, and Potawatomi).

Ice cave

offered to take my mother down the coast to the Ludington hospital, where a second cousin of father's was married to a man called "Half-Doctor." [He was an orderly at the hospital.]

This was [Nagoos e Kabbebonung Gissis] the Moon-of-the-Wild-Geese-Calling-Northward, not quite yet [Bedokwedagiming Gissis] the Moon-of-the-Breaking-of-Snowshoes [approximately March to April]. Hopeful that the magic of a white man's hospital might bring about what the magic of their love had not, Mother was bundled onto the fishing boat and they started southward. There was a strong wind out of Keewaydin [the North West], ice caves still stood along the shoreline, and ice cannonades were a threat to weaker areas of the home-hewn craft. Somewhere out on Lake Michigan, between the lumbering settlements called Frankfort and Ludington, the need for the trip ceased to exist. Under circumstances less than favorable, on a deck awash with frigid water and floating ice, I had come into this world obviously healthy and objecting loudly. The little craft turned around, putt-putting triumphantly back to our home on Cat Head Bay. Evidently, our native neighbors said, the Water Spirits had asserted the right of this child to live. If my parents did not agree, they at least did not deny this interpretation, and often they related the events surrounding my birth.

Great Aunt Susan Bpgonikwe [B-p-gon-i-kwe] made a beautiful design for my tuckanagon [cradle board] honoring the Northwest Wind (Keewaydinoodin) and the Water Spirits, but mother would not put me into it until she had added the emblems of cross and anchor.

Much later, whenever I was more boisterous than a proper Anishinaabe child should be, Wauboshtigwan would playfully remark that the first sound I'd heard was the foghorn—and I'd been blowing ever since! But he was wrong. It was the sound of great waters that I heard—would always hear. No matter what happened, the lack of that sound would plunge me into homesickness, and the background of its music would bring about a feeling of well-being and happiness. Whatever the rhythm of MishiTchgamig [Lake Michigan], it has matched the rhythm of my heart, or my heart has matched its rhythm. It is my own continued lullaby and theme song.

Another Birthing Story

The bunty [a type of boat] *Halgaa Sven* rounded the chop water at the point, then headed obliquely into the more regulated waves of the bight. Contact with each wave crest was a bounce dance of joy.

Local waterfronters, peering through the misty panes of Soren's Café, didn't see it as a dance of joy. Diving for their mackinaws, they called to Soren to save the "drift" [foam in their beer] in their glasses and bolted outside into the galelike winds of early April.

Their voices drifted back into the murky warmth: "—told 'em not to go out in this weather." "—No good to sail before th' ice balls melt. . . ." "Must be pretty bad out there for 'em to return this soon."

As they rounded the path toward the *Halgaa*'s cedar-post

dock, the apprehension changed. [Although] one cedar post had been knocked flat, the *Halgaa* was moored to the remaining posts. Flags flew from every possible projection of the craft: the red and white of *Halgaa*'s homeland, the Baltic Isles of Nord Sea; the blue and white of Sven's homeland, Sweden; the marine flag of the Great Lakes; and a multicolored bunting left over from the Fourth of July two years gone. The flags were intended to allay any fears of land watchers who knew the *Halgaa* had gone out into uncertain waters to take my mother to the Ludington hospital, where "Uncle Doctor" worked. The springtime flooded muck bogs and mires between Northport and Traverse City made travel by land quite impossible.

The rejoicing passengers were push-supported [off the boat and] toward Soren's, where Mrs. Soren, quicker to discern the meaning of the flags than the menfolk, had already prepared great bowls of steaming soup.

The trip had been curtailed suddenly when, somewhere near Point Betsie, I had decided to appear without hospital ministrations, the North Wind and I both shrieking loudly.

The rejoicing reasons may have been different, but reasons for rejoicing they were. Captain Nels Sven was ebullient about having piloted his boat, so early in the season, as far south as the Manistee and returned safely. One of the hands was bragging about his quick action in "lassoing" my mother and me with a drop net when he saw a big wave approaching. That wave washed both of us clean and also carried my placenta out into the lake. My mother was filled with quiet gladness over the birth of a healthy, normal child.

As my father hitched up Old Gray [to return home], Captain Sven joked with him about "see'n you folks around the same time again next year." Dad said, "No, never again," but my mother agreed. "Captain Sven, we've already promised for our first son to be called John, but when the second son appears, we shall call him Nels in appreciation of your valiant service to our family."

Several times, long years after, I found Mother with tears. She was remembering Nels . . . the son who didn't live to sail with Captain Sven.

Of course, I don't remember being born, but the tale of my birthing was so often repeated, I sometimes thought I did. When the "cannonballs" shoot off from the beach-bound floes and the great flocks stretch out in the Moon-of-the-Wild-Geese-Calling-Northward, there is a stirring within that has the essence of remembering.

Tuckanagon

There are things I really do remember. When I was little they used to tell me I couldn't possibly remember that far back, but I know I did. I could remember the baby clothing and the colors and the patterns and colors of the blankets our family had. Colors, especially colors, and music.

One of the first things I can remember is from the time when I was still hanging in my tuckanagon. I look down upon a clearing that is bathed in the glow of a late autumn afternoon. There is a cabin, a rain barrel, and a dog sleeping in the sun. Nearer to me is a rough table. A woman, who is not Mama, is weaving upon a large mat. Her single black braid swings across her back, and she sings in a high, clear voice as she moves rhythmically. That's all. This scene, the lovely light, and the sound. A spot memory, not a sustained one, but I can still sing the song.

Rescue

In another spot memory from that same period, I am again laced into the tuckanagon. This scene is not filled with warmth and light but with fear. Two large, feathered beings are trying to get inside the tuckanagon and scratch my eyes out. There are snarls and screams. Mother comes running from the cabin, throws up her arms, and tumbles over into a pile of mother parts. Daddy comes running, but he keeps on coming. Just when I think he will save me, he whizzes past and begins to examine something on the ground behind, crying, "My God, Oh my God!"

He carries me to mother and washes both of our faces. That Mother should need her face washed did not seem strange to me until years afterward. "Two of them," he said to my mother, "two gigantic Michimukwog [bears]; from the size and depth of their footprints, at least five feet tall." "Were they trying to eat her?" quavered Mother.

"Don't be silly," answered Father, "they were standing back of her and fighting off the hawks who were after her eyes." He stood up and scattered out the entire contents of his kinnikinnick bag [full of sacred plants used for communicating with the Blessed Spirits]. "There is no doubt they were defending their own clan blood." He hung a bear claw around my neck, and Mother did not mutter about "pagan" things. But she cried.

"Two angels," she cried, "Two angels could have done it as well as two bears. Where were they?" Mother had foresworn the Bear Clan to become an active Christian. Not that she wasn't born being one, but they have their ways of vision questing also, and she had stood beside the river and sung "Sagiima Cross NinDode-maing" ("The Holy Cross, I Take It for My Dodem Sign").

✸ ✸ ✸ ✸

My first words were "go go"—not "Mama" or "Papa" but "go go."

Punishment . . . Or . . .

Other flashbacks of remembrance come occasionally from the very earliest days of my life. One of these surrounds a punishment I was given before I was two years old—at least, that's what I *thought* it was for many years. Retrospect has given it quite another slant.

The remembered scene is a warm, sunlit day on a Lake Michigan beach, where the expanse of water continues into infinity. Brilliant sun flashes glint off the crests of gentle waves, and my mother and father and I are sporting in the waters. The first part of the recall is bathed with great warmth and happiness. My father "rides" me around on his back. Then he floats, and I sit on his stomach, bouncing with laughter. I discover how to splash and sparkle my mother all over. The big, shiny droplets run slowly down her long, black hair and glisten in the sun. I call them "Mama's beads."

I sit on hard, rippled sand and toss little stones. Stones already know how to splash; nobody has to show them how. At this point, my parents fade from the picture. I try to catch a crayfish. He waves his pincers and makes me laugh. I want him to make some kind of noise. All the other animals I know have special sounds of their own.

Then I wonder what is going on underwater, so I wade out and sit down on the bottom. I really like it down here. A beautiful, green gloom is everywhere; it does not put hurts in my eyes as the sunlight did. A school of shiny, darting fish swim across my tummy. Some wavy plants tickle my legs, and a round fish with a target on his cover nibbles at my toes. Everything is especially wonderful. Suddenly I discover a tiny silver nest kept by an enchanted silver fish with stickles on his back. That miniature nest and its animated guardian so enthrall me that I will recall this moment with clarity for the rest of my life. My magic fishling is just nosing a shiny ball into the net of his nest when my submarine reverie is abruptly ended.

I am unexpectedly and rudely catapulted high above the water by an unseen power! At first, I do not recognize the source of the force—only that I am angered by the violent interruption—but soon the voice sounds that accompany the removal tell me that it is my father, Wauboshtigwan.

"Ka, Ka! Matchi-abinodji. Kawessa mika! No, no! Bad girl. Never again do that! The Water Spirits are not our kind."

He throws me on the ground, squashing my face in the sand and spanking me hard on the back. Water pops up in my nose and runs out of my mouth. Next I am spanked on my front. I begin to cough and then to kick and cry loudly. Mother forsakes me and runs away. As if the first spankings were not enough, Father now cuts a gigantic stick from the water willows and wallops me on the behind. Much of what he is saying I do not understand, but his meaning is abundantly clear. He does not wish me to have fun on the bottom of the lake anymore. He will hurt me very badly if I ever try to play down there again.

Mother returns with the beautiful-mustn't-touch-medicine-bag-which-hangs-up-in-the-rafters. She will love me. No, Mother is acting very strangely also. Together, she and Father wade out and throw little things upon the surface of the lake, murmuring unintelligible words.[2]

Up to that moment, feelings of joy and security had always flooded over me whenever I heard my daddy's voice. But now apprehension had been added to those feelings. Now I sensed that Wauboshtigwan would not ALWAYS give me everything I wanted. The days of perfection were over, and I had begun to grow up, but it would be a protracted childhood time before I also understood that what I wanted was not always best for me.

When I Became a Mother

Fifteen years into the future I REALLY understood what had happened that day. Grandmother Sauganash [Englishman] had sent our boys some civilized swimming trunks, a gentle hint, no doubt, that she did not wish to see them naked when she came to visit. The trunks were bright red, blue, and yellow and pleased the boys immensely. At first they thought they were "party pants" and were surprised to find that it was all right to get them wet!

"How come you and Daddy don't gets any, Muvver?" Shay laughed and said Daddy was going to wear his old overalls so that he could work on the bottom of the old boat on the beach. I

---

2. They were murmuring words of gratitude to the Blessed Spirits for the safety of their young daughter.

slipped a clip knife into my smock pocket in case the spear reeds were ripe.

It was a lovely afternoon. Shay splashed in the water a bit and then began scraping the old hull. The boys were red, blue, and yellow blurs as they raced up and down the shore, occasionally jumping into the water and squealing. Finding that the condition of the spear reeds was ideal, I swam to the sand spit and harvested a great armful. I had just begun to separate the tops for weaving and the root tips for salad when I realized that a sound was missing from the music of the Summer Bay Symphony. It was the voice of wee Stevie.

I think I flew to the pile of sunken deadheads beyond the spit; I've no memory of traveling there. The drawstrings on Stevie's little yellow "party pants" had caught on a snag and held him under.

As I threw the beloved little body onto the beach, cleaned out the mouth and nostrils, and bubbled the water from his lungs, the process merged with another day of long ago.

Suddenly I felt my father's hands and heard his voice crying. "The Water Spirits are not our kind!" So that was it! What I had thought of, all those years, as an undeserved punishment from a strict patriarch had actually been an act of great love and great fear.

Remembering how it had been for me, I did not spank wee Stevie, although we had often warned the boys away from the deadhead pile. Instead I hugged him hard, and the water on his little shoulders was not all from the lake.

"You hurtind me, Muvver." So I had done it anyway—and the memory process had gone full cycle in reality.

Did Wauboshtigwan have more reason to fear for the life of his child than I? At the time I had thought so, but little did I know. Then I was a woman in body only, not in experience, not in mind, not in spirit. A lengthy Sun Trail of living was ahead before these should be accomplished.[3]

---

3. The Sun Trail guides us on our path as we move from the East to West, striving to Walk in Balance and Honor upon Mother Earth.

A Young Girl,
Close to Aki (Mother Earth)

Baby Naming

My parents had agreed that their children should be brought up with
the knowledge of all faiths so that they could wisely make their own
choices as adults. It was for this reason that I was neither christened
nor named when the time of the blueberry harvest approached. Several times the village mashkiki [medicine man] had admonished my
father that an Indian child should be named before the first nine
months. Having heard no more about it, he supposed the matter had
been taken care of by my Christian grandfather.

No prudent Anishinaabe ignores the pleasure and benefits of
the Blueberry Moon [roughly August, depending on when the full
moon occurs] and my parents were among the most prudent. I was
left suspended in a blanket nest while they harvested—safe
because I could not walk, or so they thought. On one return to the
blanket area to empty buckets, they found I was gone. A short
investigation revealed me standing between two bears. They were
pulling blueberries into their giant maws, and so was I.

My parents hurriedly agreed to wait silently until the bears disappeared and they would rush in to grab their baby. When the
bears left, baby grabbed hold of bear hair on either side and went
along! Chastised again by the appearance of bears for a second
time, my parents took me to the local mashkiki, who refused to
give me a naming.

"I should be sacrilegious to do such a thing," he said, "when the blessed Blueberries, who have always sustained Our People, and the Spirits of MichiMukwog [Sacred Bears] have already named her. No matter what you or I should say, people would always call her 'Walks-With-Bears.'" And so they did.

Until the Grand Midé called my adult name to the seven directions, I was MUKWOGBIMOSINIM, "Walks-With-Bears-Girl."

Anyone Around Clearing

I recall this one time when I was very, very little, just how little I don't know because the world is very big when you are very little. Neither do I know how important this really was, but it was a big happening in my tiny life. I ran away.

I'd overheard some adults quarreling. I don't know who was quarreling nor what they were quarreling about. I just know that it wounded me, whatever it was. So I ran away. I don't how far I went, but in my childish view it was long way that I ran on the path. At last I came to a clearing with a great big stone in the middle of it. I stopped there. I walked around the great stone.

A Voice said, "What are you doing here?"

I answered, "I am running away."

"From what do you run?"

"There are happenings going on back at the house. I can't stay there anymore. I don't like it."

Then the Voice said, "We understand. But it's all right now. Go home."

I just stood there.

Then the Voice said, "What are you doing here?" Replay. (But of course I didn't think of it as replay.)

Again I said, "I'm running away."

Three times. The third or fourth time the Voice was rather cross and said, "It's all right, now!"

I'm afraid I was impudent, not having been taught at that tender age how to respectfully address spirit beings. "So how do I know? Just because You say so. . . . I can't even see You! Huh!"

There was a stony sigh of eonic impatience. "Well, go and see, and then you will know." That seemed sensible. So I went back to see. I wasn't at all sure I could go back, but I did eventually.

My mother said, "Wherever have you been?"

"A looong way."

"Don't you do it again without Mother or Daddy going with you."

Then I asked, "Who is it that talks Out There?"

The parents replied, " Oh, anybody that's around."

For several years I called that place Anybody Around Clearing.

Parents

Some people now don't know anything about their relatives, but these were things that I was told for entertainment. I would say to my mother, "Tell me about when you were a little girl. Tell me about what it was like at Wyncobank.[1] Tell me about the time you got stuck in the door with the pig." I used to beg my dad to tell me stories about the time when he was overseas because it seemed wonderfully exciting to me. My mother sometimes didn't like me to ask about that because she thought that there were a lot of guns and fighting. I don't think she dreamed, along with the people of her generation, of how awful the world situation was going to get by comparison.

☩ ☩ ☩ ☩

Nearly every parent, I notice, wishes for his offspring whatever good he thinks he has missed in his own life. So it was with my parents; so it has been with me.

---

1. Wyncobank was the ancestral home in England of Francis Hague Blackman Moorhouse.

Wauboshtigwan and Minosoahnikwe wanted me to have a superlative education. For many years, I supposed their reason to be security. I thought they saw in education social and financial security—and the possibility of a husband with a professional occupation. I certainly received that impression. Looking back now, I see that I would not have escaped education either formally or informally, for the one great common denominator in the ancestral lines of BOTH my parents was an eternal intellectual curiosity—an undeniable love of knowledge, simply for the joy of knowing.

✳ ✳ ✳ ✳

Ni Mishomis Sauganash (which means "Grandfather Englishman" in Anishinaabemowin) was the Reverend Francis Blackman Moorhouse. He had deliberately chosen to leave the comforts of a Yorkshire manor [in England] in order to bring the light of salvation to the benighted native of the American backcountry. This never deterred him from studying and writing voluminously. He considered his expenditures for books to be his besetting sin! Even when he was ninety-seven and could scarcely walk, he sat in the sun of the apple orchard with the cat on one knee and a volume of Josephus in New Testament Greek on the other. "Puss" would follow the light point of Grandfather's magnifying glass as it moved across the page, and it looked as if pussycat were reading too!

Ni Mishomis MidéOgema (My Grandfather Who-Leads-in-the-Grand-Medicine) [Anishinaabeg spiritual teachings] recited the cycle of his oral traditions religiously throughout the changes of seasons, whether devoted followers were present or not, never ceasing to chant, pray, and fast for revelation and understanding. To his dying day, he observed the lessons of the natural world as carefully as he had when he was first a warrior and physical safety depended on it. He would climb the western dunes and examine the evening sky in order to determine activities for the next day. It was his idea of efficiency.

Sometimes when he returned home and reported, "Gitchi

Manidu [Creator/Great Spirit] say no point in planning to do wash tomorrow," my mother would be greatly irked and mutter something under her breath about needing clean clothes, Gitchi Manidu or not. But MidéOgema's reports were never incorrect.

Very early I accepted the fact that both my grandfathers had an extra special "in" with the Supreme Being. The methods of these two were at variance, but the intellectual search was the same.

My parents had become acquainted on the long walk to a one-room rural school. By now, truly only heaven knows how many months those two had walked the country lane together, the lonely pale boy who recognized every bird, animal, plant, and tree as a personal friend and the dark, independent girl who understood about the behavior of people so early in life. No one ever knew, not even they themselves, at what point that friendship developed into a devotion [to each other] that never failed as long as they lived. Certainly the first to surmise this was the teacher of that remote schoolhouse, one Langely Scott by name. God bless his perspicacity!

He must have been a crackerjack of a teacher. When Mr. Scott lay dying of cancer [in his last years], people from all over came to see him. My mother and father were amazed that he knew so many people.

One day, as Father handed over mother's lunch pail and book bag at the schoolhouse gate, Mr. Scott came to meet her and inquired why her friend did not attend the school.

"Oh, he does go to school," my mother said, "but in the old Indian way. He learns daily from his father and uncles, not only the ways of the woods, but long legends and songs of his people, how to bring the rain, plant crops, and follow the Sun Trail. He is a very deep thinker," she added proudly.

Mr. Scott gave young Sarah, for so she was called then, a searching look.

"A philosopher at fifteen? Not the usual." Then he added, "But that boy's being Indian is even more unlikely."

15

"Oh, he knows about that," Sarah answered brightly, "he looks that way [pale] because his mother's father [James Moray] was Scottish—a merchantman wrecked on the Whiskey Island reef, he says." Mr. Scott didn't believe it at first, but he checked with old Ettawageeshik about the wreck. That part was true enough, and he also found out that the lone survivor had married Cecilia Manidu, commonly called Kishawish. Kitiganing Indians, paddling back from drying fish on Fishing Island (now called Gull Island), had picked the near lifeless body of James Moray out of the wreckage.

All our relatives and neighbors delighted in hearing my father tell about his Scottish grandfather. He would crush mother's round sofa pillow onto his head, tie a towel about his middle, clench a long stick between his teeth, and drawl, "Went ter sleep in'ta dour cauld glam, ah deed, n'oped t'eye in't warrum arrums uv youn Kishawish. Tha munna dinna ken but t'fool t'wud move awa'." [I went to sleep in the dark cold water, I did, and opened my eyes in the warm arms of young Kishawish. You know no one but a fool would have moved away.] Everyone would collapse with hysterical merriment.

Mother once told me that she surmised that when this teacher, Langely Scott, first extended himself to help Father, he thought he was "rescuing" a white boy brought up by the Indians. Father was then called by his boyhood name of Wessee.

Whatever the joint reasons and effort of Sarah and Mr. Scott, they brought Wessee into the world of the school, where Mr. Scott changed the name of Wessee Pakkawakkuk to Wesley Cook and soon convinced the boy he needed to know something of the white man's world in order to get along in life. How much "getting along in life" also involved getting along with the beautiful Sarah one can but conjecture, but the thought must have figured prominently in his mind! Be that as it may, when Sarah passed her eighth-grade examinations at the top of the class, Wessee passed them too—at the bottom of the class. It was nevertheless a pass and a truly remarkable feat for a boy who only a year before had never read a book nor held a pen.

Wessee showed a real flair for writing, especially in the florid Victorian style so popular at the time. He may not have used the pen before, but the transfer to pen and ink from stylus and birchbark was not as great as Mr. Scott preferred to believe. In a short time, Wessee was famous for his penmanship; in fact, he made out the certificates for the graduating class.

An eighth-grade education was about all anyone in their community ever expected to achieve. Graduation from the school was a big affair, complete with new clothes, diplomas, recitations, and refreshments. A photographer came from nearby Brown City to make formal photographs.[2]

One look at Sarah and he decided she must become a photographer's model—his. When the photographer met Grandfather Sauganash, however, that gentleman was not only wearing his best clergyman's suit but also projected his best ministerial personality. Quickly the photographer changed his intended offer [of modeling] into teaching Sarah the art of photography. This offer Grandfather accepted with dignity, believing it to be the guiding hand of God and little realizing the complication ahead for Sarah in trying to escape the hands of the photographer!

When Mr. Scott received prints of the formal photographs for orders from graduates' families, he also received a number of informal shots taken in the schoolyard. Among these was one of the intended model and her swain surrounded by springtime. A single look at the print of Sarah and Wessee holding hands under the schoolyard apple tree sent Grandfather Sauganash into a near panic. (He actually did become ill a year later when the photo appeared in a Detroit rotogravure to advertise Pear Soap.)

Carrying gifts like the proverbial Greek, Grandfather Sauganash called upon Grandfather MidéOgema in his lodge. He was impressed by the courtesy with which he was received. Midé-Ogema and the Reverend Francis Moorhouse had conferred with their sacred objects. The two men talked together for a long time, actually enjoying each other's company and finding themselves in

2. Brown City is located in Sanilac County in southeastern Michigan.

complete agreement on one matter at least. Sarah and Wessee were forbidden to see each other again. The disparate cultures, in spite of both being Anishinaabeg, made them undesirable mates for each other. In those days, well brought up young people of both cultures did as their fathers directed. So twenty years later, when Sarah and Wessee finally came together, it was with an intensity of delight that lasted for the remainder of their lifetimes.

Sarah went to work in the photographer's shop at Brown City. She was paid the magnificent sum of three dollars per week and her room and board. For this, she was expected to assist the photographer's wife, who was chronically "ailing," with the housework [and] do the dishes and some of the ironing. At the photo shop, she made appointments, "kept shop," did the touch-up work on negatives, mounted photographs, arranged and changed the display windows, dusted, cleaned, mopped, tallied up the receipts at the close of the day, made and served coffee, prepared customers for photography, [and] polished the lenses and other photographic equipment so that they were constantly in immaculate condition. She was seventeen years old.

Simultaneously, Wessee committed himself as a hired hand to a local farmer. He undertook to perform all the field work with horses on 650 acres of land. In exchange for this, he was to receive [sleeping] accommodations in the barn, meals five days a week, and at the end of the year title to 20 acres of land. No money. It was a good thing for him that he had learned from his family how to find wild edibles [to augment his frugal diet]. At the end of that year, Father had ceremonially left behind him the name of Wessee and become Wauboshtigwan [having successfully completed his life's vision quest]. He had also become a walking skeleton held together by bulging muscles, the legal owner of 20 acres [and] a mustache, and [was] five inches taller.

My father was absolutely exalted, getting this land. He walked out of the land office in Valley Center with the deed to the land, the whole world beautiful and rosy, until the man stuck his head out and said, "Oh, by the way, I forgot, here's the taxes."

My dad said, "What's this?"

He replied, "Well, 'this' is the taxes you have to pay on the land."

My dad said, "Who do I have to pay them to?"

The man said, "Well, you have to pay it to the county."

My dad responded, "I can't pay this [in cash], I've already paid for the land by working on it."

The man said, "This is different. This [tax] comes every year. You have to pay it [in cash] regularly."

Being inexperienced as a landholder, Wauboshtigwan had not understood about taxes. He was plunged into despair when he found out these must be paid or one loses the land. He didn't understand about it at all, so he went to see the police. He figured they ought to know the legality of things.

He said, "I don't understand these taxes." Sure enough, the man at the land office had been right. Every single year, even though you own the land, you have to pay it.

"What happens if I can't pay for it?"

They told him, "They take the land away from you!"

In the midst of his dismay, he saw an advertisement for the U.S. Marine Corps. Underneath it said that in exchange for so much time in the service they'd get paid twenty gold pieces, all the clothing they needed, and all the room and board they needed.

He went into the office and said, "This can't be right." They pointed out to him exactly what it was, showing him the kind of clothing. He asked how long he'd have to do this. When he signed up, he got a beautiful blue coat with red lining and brass buttons.

He really felt very splendid in it. And he got twenty gold pieces. Of course, he had to show up [to serve], but because he got the twenty gold pieces he went and paid the taxes right away.

As Wauboshtigwan's departure for service [in the Spanish-American War] became imminent, a sort of groundswell pressure to let the two meet again expressed itself from the community. Honoring the dictates of their parents, Sarah and Wauboshtigwan had not seen each other for a year.

Later, on their tenth wedding anniversary, they admitted slyly that they *had* exchanged notes during that time. Across from the schoolhouse gate there was a hollow fencepost where once a blue-bird nested, and they had left information there for each other during the dinner-pail years. Aided and abetted by no less an unlikely cupid than Langely Scott, they continued to use the old post as a place to exchange letters.

"You can't keep those young people apart. After all," the church elders said to my minister grandfather, "with the lad going off to the Spanish Wars, he may never come back again. If'n the cannon don't git 'im, the malaria will. God rest 'is soul."

The cannon didn't git 'im. The malaria didn't git 'im. Neither did the typhoid, the venomous snakes, nor the poisonous spiders.

Before the people who enlisted marched away, my mother and father got to see each other . . . at the park in the middle of Valley Center, with the whole village there.

My dad and his younger brother traveled around the world. My dad wrote sometimes to my mother but not a great deal. My mother worried because both her father and her cousins in Detroit kept parading men in front of her, but none of them came up to Wessee.

Meanwhile, every Friday, promptly at five o'clock in the afternoon, Grandfather Sauganash pulled up his horse and buggy in front of the shop to take his daughter home for the weekend. Each week Sarah gave one dollar to her father toward running the farm, while fifty cents was unobtrusively dropped into her mother's "chicken money" can, one dollar was put into the bank, and fifty cents was retained toward the expenses of the coming week.

Several times Sarah tried to talk with her father about her problems with the amorous Mr. Brown [the photographer], but that reverend gentleman was of the opinion that God defends the innocent and one receives behavioral response in kind as one offers. If she acted with propriety and modesty, esteem and respect would be accorded her in return. Since continuous examination of her own motives and concentrated prayer did not seem to have much effect upon Mr. Brown, Sarah came to the conclusion that she would have to look for another job on her own, and this she began to do.

When she saw that things just weren't working out, she wrote to her cousin Sarah, who lived in Detroit. She was another one of the Sarahs. There were seven Moorhouse boys, and they all named their first girl after their mother . . . so they were all 'Sarah'. They wound up with relatives all over the world with names like Big Sarah, Little Sarah, Black Sarah, and Red Sarah.

She wrote to her cousin and said, "I can't stay here, and I can't talk to my parents about the situation, but I've had a couple of real narrow escapes. I have to get out of here." Cousin Sarah talked to her parents, and, although they already had a whole house full of people, they agreed for her to [come and stay with them]. Because this was his own brother, her father agreed that she could go there, but he didn't like it.

Sarah, having found a new job retouching photographs in a Detroit gallery, began to fear that the old Wessee was disappearing. [A stranger peered out at her from a photo taken] on the docks of Ceylon, one who sent a carved ivory fan, selected with the help of the captain's lady, and who wore a pigeon blood ruby around his neck.

Of course, she did not realize how much she had changed herself. Partly because of the salary, she had become more and more of a model and less a photographic assistant. Ladies' hats were *unbelievable* creations at that time. She began to model hats, then to design them, and was told she had a "natural flair" for millinery. Clothing manufacturers began to offer her their lines if she would be seen in them at the right places. It seemed a simple enough thing to do, especially since the younger children at home had begun to go to college and more money was needed.

She had one beau whom she kind of liked. But she couldn't marry him because he was a [Roman] Catholic. And one of the sculptors, named Fortunati, had a real case on her. She had several pieces of jewelry from him, which she always cherished. But she decided, under the circumstances [since she didn't love him], that it would never do. It wouldn't be fair to him and it wouldn't be fair to her, but she said he was a real gentleman and she liked him very much.

[Years later] I asked her if my dad knew about it, and she said, "No, and don't you tell him." It wasn't that there were any promises exchanged between them or anything like that, but she knew he would be envious. I had reason, as an adult, to know that that was so.

Time and more money went down the drain. Grandfather Sauganash always carried the dream of becoming a successful farmer, but he never quite made it. He kept losing all his cows. They kept dying, and they didn't know what from. So she had to take an extra job because the regular money she sent home was for the two younger girls to go to college. They were both going to be teachers. It was the income from his wife's chickens, his small ministerial salary—and Sarah—that carried them along. When he sent an urgent message to Sarah because the [live]stock on the farm had [mysteriously] begun to die off, she then took on an evening job posing as a designer's model for religious statuary. She always felt a little guilty about this job but justified the situation to herself by thinking that, since it was somewhat associated with religion, it must have its virtuous aspect. Besides, when she was overtired from a day in the millinery shop or didn't feel well, they said she looked more soulful and even paid more money! All she had to do was stand there and move to different positions.

✠ ✠ ✠ ✠

MidéOgema swaggered openly when he went to town. It was a delightful experience to him—being admired by white men because of his son in the service.

"Old innian medicine plenty strong stuff, you bet. Make medicine now to get boy much eagle feather." A month after his father was heard to make this statement, Wauboshtigwan was decorated for bravery! He had dived into the Mindanao Deep and untangled an anchor chain that was "hopelessly" twisted into a coral reef, thereby saving the fleet's flagship and all aboard. Any kid raised on the Great Lakes islands could have done it. There was no special diving equipment during the time of the Spanish-American War.

The local townsfolk were all agape, for Father's picture had been in all of the mainland papers; a smartly uniformed, debonair stranger looked out from the photograph taken on the deck.

[Later] during World War II, my dad was listening to the radio about the fall of Bananga Point, which fell after Corregidor.

He kept saying, "No way could a plane possibly get a bomb in there. Somebody must have given up!"

Everybody would say, "What do you mean, they 'can't'? How do you know what it's like? This is the Caribbean not the Great Lakes."

He said, "I put those fortifications in there! I was in the Philippines!"

One day, as Father was directing a crew fortifying Bananga Point,[3] a body of armed guards approached. He came to attention, saluted, and waited for their message. The message was incredible. He was suspected of sending and receiving messages from an unknown enemy. Promptly, he was marched off to headquarters.

A piece of birchbark lay on top of the shiny mahogany table. Father wondered to himself what a piece of birchbark could possibly be doing in the Philippines. He stepped closer. Incised into the first layer of the bark was a message in Ojibway hieroglyphs.[4] Father laughed, but the laughter fell on cold, unsympathetic ears.

---

3. Bananga Point, in the Philippines, is where Wesley Cook (Wauboshtigwan) completed his military service.

4. Hieroglyphs are used to convey messages and as memory aids. This is a sample of hieroglyphs taken from *Min: Anishinaabeg Ogimaawi-minan BlueBerry: First Fruit of The People,* 26, stories collected and retold by Keewaydinoquay and published by the Miniss Kitigan Drum in 1978.

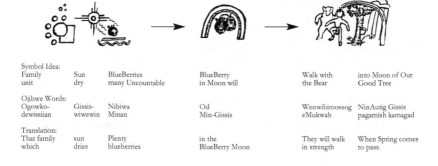

Symbol Idea:					
Family	Sun	BlueBerries	BlueBerry	Walk with	into Moon of Our
unit	dry	many Uncountable	in Moon will	the Bear	Good Tree
Ojibwe Words:					
Ogowko-	Gissis-	Nibiwa	Od	Wenwibimossog	NinAutig Gissis
dewissiian	wiwewin	Minan	Min-Gissis	eMukwah	pagamish kamagad
Translation:					
That family	sun	Plenty	in the	They will walk	When Spring comes
which	dries	blueberries	BlueBerry Moon	in strength	to pass.

23

"You can interpret this insidious message?" demanded the supervising officer.

"It is not insidious, sir."

"Ah, then you *can* interpret it."

"Yessir."

"Do so."

Father looked uncomfortable. "It will seem foolish to you. It's just a message about things at home from my father."

"Perhaps you do not understand your position. You are suspected of infiltrating communications with subversive material. Interpret."

Father flipped over the birchbark. "This is not subversive communication. It is an item of the United States mail, cut to standard size, duly stamped, and addressed in the hand of Gustava Soren, who keeps the post office in the grocery store at Mellon's Corners in Michigan."

"Interpret."

There was no mistaking the hard anger in the voice. So Father took a deep breath and interpreted . . .

make a white man's letter to your heart's woman
say through her that the people of the islands
salute the chief of her lodge with all respect
say that praying to great spirit is always good
but works better on cows if poison plants are
pulled with roots out of lower pasture

[Many years passed.] One weekend, nearly twenty years later, when my mom was at home visiting her parents, her father called her into his study and asked her, "Do you still hear from Wessee?"

She said, "Not very often."

He said, "Does he still want to marry you?"

She said, "I don't know. You told us not to talk about it." My father and mother were thirty-seven and thirty-five years old. Neither of them had been married before.

So my grandfather said, "Your mother and I have talked this over. Now you're thirty-five years old, and probably nobody else would want you. If he still wants to marry you, we have agreed between us that we would allow that. We don't like it, but we would agree to it." They'd done their best, parading all these men in front of her and taking her to church meetings and whatnot. My mother had found nobody at these affairs; [in fact,] she spent most of her time trying to escape them, and [judging] from the advice she gave me later she probably did.

So my dad resigned his commission and bought a diamond ring. It was a good diamond. It sparkled across the room. He came home, and they were married twice. My missionary grandfather married them in his church, and MidéOgema had a traditional wedding ceremony and a sweat for them up north.

When they did finally come together, it was with an intensity of delight that would last a lifetime.

✶ ✶ ✶ ✶

[And yet they did not always agree about everything.] My mother was afraid that he was going to just make a career of the military. When my father came home, he had two socks—two old socks—which he had darned extra hard so they would be firm, and they were filled solid with silver pieces. You couldn't lift them. My father was [so] frugal that he went down to the beach and played with the crabs while the other [soldiers] were having a good time spending all their money in town—and that sort of thing.

Anyway, he went all over the world, and he used to tell me about all these places he visited. It was really enchanting to me. He bought things. He bought my mother a little box with inlaid mother-of-pearl in the top of it in the Philippines. He bought all kinds of things we considered exotic because then people didn't have a chance to buy things from faraway places like they do now.

Tea box with an inlaid mother-of-pearl design and some brass buttons from Wessee's Marine uniform

And then, I don't know exactly how, my mother persuaded my father to sell that land in Valley Center that he had worked for, and they used the money to go to college.

They went to college, and they'd been there almost a month, and the dean called them in and said "Sorry, your records haven't come through." When he asked them what high school they'd graduated from, they said, well, they never did graduate from high school.

He said, "You can't go to college if you didn't graduate from high school!" They didn't know this.

So the dean of the school of MSU [Michigan State University], which in those days was Michigan Agricultural College [MAC], told them that they should go to Big Rapids, where there was a college—today it's a pharmaceutical college, but it used to be just for people who needed to pick up some credits they were short in or for people who'd flunked out someplace else or something like that. He told them to go there for a year, and he told them what courses to take and said if they did well, why, they could come back.

So they had to move out of the place they were in and find another place in another town and start college there. And of course they did well. The following year they went back to Michigan Agricultural College in East Lansing, Michigan. They helped to form the first married student association anywhere because people didn't get married and go to school then. It was a very unusual thing. They finished college there at MAC.

My mother didn't ever get a degree. She just took a lot of courses and then she quit. But my father got a degree in horticulture. He even got honors.

He had a thing for trees from the very beginning. When he first got out he took a job as a county agricultural agent. Then he got into some sort of business deal, which folded. They lost the store [that they owned] and the house they lived in.

The Great Depression

I've never been able to understand how it was that a bank that failed could take their house and their business and there was still money [owed to the bank], which my parents were supposed to pay back. But when they closed, they [still] had my parents' bank account, which the bank never paid back, and apparently that's what could happen then. They should at least have called it even. By then, my parents were without resources. So I imagine that's why they moved back to the woods.

They had a good time [there, though]. They had a lot of good friends, who kept coming to see them. They always put on that this was their choice, to live this way. But I don't think so now. I think they just couldn't do anything else. They moved from one place to another. That's probably why my ambition for my kids was that they should each have a piece of land that was their own . . . a place they could call home. To me that was the most important thing. I've seen a lot of people come home, and there's no home to come to . . . people who've sold off the old farm. . . .

My dad had a job, but it wasn't what some people think of as a job. Trees were his first love. There was no doubt about it. He would go anywhere that a tree was in trouble, and he was very good at it. He looked at it as being a tree doctor. I mean, he felt that way. No one else did, but he would bind up a tree and fix its hurts.

We'd be buzzing along the highway in our old Model T Ford, and all of a sudden my dad would pull over, and my mother would say, "What now? Another flat tire?"

And he'd say, "No, have to fix a tree." Then he'd be off to work on some tree.

I think my mother felt like trees were his first love. It wasn't a proper thing for a good Indian wife to say, but I think she thought it.

I remember one time I ran in and I said, "Where's my father, he has to come right now!"

And she said, "I don't know where he is. He's off with some tree somewhere."

"But," I said, "we need him right now because the calf is coming right now!"

And she said, "That's too bad. I can't tell you where he is."

I said, "But you know I can't hold it, and neither can you! And that calf probably shouldn't hit the floor so it won't break anything!" We finally got some things, some old tarps and stuff like that, [to cushion the calf] so it wouldn't break any bones.

But I remember her saying, "Well, how should I know where he is? He's off with a tree somewhere."

It was true. He'd fix trees. He'd go onto other people's properties and fix trees, and he would say, "I'm just climbing up. Just give me enough time to fix this limb."

And they would say, "I'm not going to pay you for that."

Then he'd say, "Well, I didn't expect you to."

Sometimes in the Spring the winds would have twisted a limb off one tree, and he'd just love to take one kind of tree and graft it onto another where a limb had been wrested off or there was an opening of some kind. He loved to do that. We had a plum tree in a garden in one place where we lived. He had red and yellow and green and purple plums, [all] on that same tree. It didn't show so much with the flowers. But he'd take people out there to show 'em.

I never saw him so happy—on such a high—as he was when he'd take somebody out and say, "Take a plum."

And they'd look and say, "Hey . . . there's something funny . . ." and he'd come in the house just roaring with laughter.

My parents also had some cattle. They used to have chickens, but after they ate up my mother's whole garden one time—she had to replant the whole thing in July—she said, "Now either you build a new chicken yard or we're not going to have chickens." Well, we went without chickens for a long time, and that wasn't so good. Chicken was my favorite food. You can catch a chicken a lot easier than you can catch a cow and carve a steak off of it. . . .

My dad hated to hunt. I remember my mother shoving the gun into his hand and saying, "Go get some meat. I need something to cook on the stove. You're trying to tell me that you were with the United States Marine Corps, but you can't go out there and shoot a partridge?" My dad would go, feet lagging.

※ ※ ※ ※

My mother had an unusual upbringing for someone living in the wilds of northern Michigan. Having spent the first years of her life in genteel England, with the manners and civilities that go along with living on a large estate and a mother who had been to finishing school, she usually ended up as the social arbiter in whatever town and section we lived in. She knew just where the salt cellars and the extra spoons and the pickle fork should go.

My mother also knew how to provide for her family, with large gardens and drying and canning food. She was especially good at weaving and kept reeds and other weaving materials handy in the little pond close by. She wove beautiful black ash baskets and some really large things such as room dividers, and a special chair for my father. My mother's fingers were always callused and red, but she could make almost anything. She worked with birchbark, reeds, rushes, plants, grasses, willows, osiers, and cedar bark and black ash.

It is from the Indian side of her family that I inherited the recipe for the ointment called Wild Cat. It is very powerful and must be used with great care to keep it out of eyes and noses. But it really works well for sore muscles and bruises. There was a lumber camp a few miles away, and on Saturday nights the lumberjacks would get to drinking and fighting just for fun. They would come to my mother to treat their bruises and gashes week after week after week. They were grateful to her and fixed up our place with many additions to make life easier and more pleasant for her.

29

My mother wove everything you can think of. She did room partitions for resorters, made baskets from here to heaven and back, trays, wastepaper baskets, and what-all. My father was tending trees, planting trees, relocating trees, bringing in produce that he found. We had so many bushels of apples we fed pigs on them. He didn't like to shoot anything but did come in with things he'd shot. He kept looking for jobs and would tell people he had a college education.

People would look at him and say, "Spell Constantinople."

✳ ✳ ✳ ✳

My father was very light. He had white skin and white hair from a very early age. He used to try to darken it [his skin] by not wearing shirts and hats and by jumping into cold water, while my mother was dark skinned and used to try to lighten her skin by always wearing hats and bonnets and long sleeves.

✳ ✳ ✳ ✳

I still have a spill dish [for placing small rolls and twists of paper used to light candles and pipes and such in after they were used, so they wouldn't accidentally start a fire] that belonged to my mother, Sarah. It came with her from England. With it came a story. . . .

It seems that when my great-grandmother, Elizabeth Pickering, would come to see my mother after she was in bed, Granny Elizabeth would put out the candle and talk with her a bit.

One night she came and she said, "Now, Sarah Elizabeth, I need to tell you something and you must listen carefully, for I can't tell you again. This is the last time I will be able to come and put you to bed. After tonight, you must be a grownup girl and do it yourself. And if sometimes you don't feel exactly like a grownup you can at least pretend to be one." Then she gave Sarah a little dish to keep her spills in. The next day my mother found out that her grandmother could not possibly have come to see her and given her the spill dish because she had already died a few days earlier.

My mother didn't often speak of supernatural things, but she looked me right in the eye and told me that she did see and talk with Grandmother Elizabeth and was given the spill dish by her that night and that she couldn't explain it but it happened.

(As told to Lee Boisvert circa 1988)

ISLE OF THE TRUE HEARTED WOMAN

True Heart was the young wife of an ambitious man, ambitious in the sense that he desired prestige, wealth, and easy living. He was NOT ambitious at working or hunting. This fact was noted by almost everyone but True Heart, who admired her handsome husband and did not seem to mind slaving to keep him in the style to which he wished to become accustomed. Her efforts were not entirely satisfactory to Ambitious Man, however, for the extra efforts required of her soon made her thin and tired, and besides she appeared to be barren.

On a trip to the mainland, the roving eye of Ambitious Man fell upon the attractive daughter of an Odawa drum chief. She was plump and pretty, and the social prominence of her father assured that a handsome dowry would become the property of her husband. Pretty Partridge seemed to enjoy the attentions of Ambitious Man, so he applied to the council of elders for permission to take a second wife. The council of elders were aware that the display of elegance and plenitude in the lodge of Ambitious Man was due to the extreme efforts of True Heart. (Their women had seen her sneaking off to the traplines in the gray light of dawn so that no one would know Ambitious Man had not filled the cooking pots of his own household.) The council told Ambitious Man that he was not really supporting one wife; therefore, they could hardly grant him permission to have two women. Ambitious Man was enraged and frustrated. He was determined to have Pretty Partridge and her dowry.

Now it happened at this time that True Heart had gone over to the Women's Island alone, for all the other young women were pregnant.[5] Only the medicine woman knew that True Heart also carried the hope of a child next to her heart.

"You must put on a sweet face and go to the Women's Island anyway," the medicine woman had told her, "for complete rest is the only way you can continue to carry this child you have so long desired. Keep very warm, put up your feet, sleep all you can. I myself will give you provisions for a nourishing broth laced with virtuous herbs."

When he supposed her time was up, Ambitious Man, feigning kindliness and consideration, took his own canoe to collect his wife from Women's Island. Fuming to himself in his lonely lodge, Ambitious Man had thought upon a plan, which he now put into effect. Pulling up beside the women's canoe at the tying-up log, he slashed the little bark until it sank, then turned and paddled back toward Kitiganing, leaving the unfortunate True Heart marooned.

All the villagers knew about the affair was that True Heart's man had come back alone, bloody and bruised, daubed with charcoal of mourning, and telling a strange story. The Women's Island, he said, was now inhabited by strange, vicious Matchi-Manidog (Evil Spirits) who wanted the island all for themselves. On arrival there, he had found the body of his poor wife impaled and horribly mutilated. The Matchi-Manidog had released him from a similar fate only because they wished him to tell the Indians to stay away. Quite terrified, they did!

After the briefest possible mourning period for his supposedly dead wife, Ambitious Man brought Pretty Partridge and

5. It was the custom, in the days when all of our people followed the native religion, for a woman to go apart from her family and the village at the time of her monthly flowing. When the weather was at all favorable, most of the local Anishinaabikweg spent their "time apart" on the small island which lies northwest of Kitiganing Island. For this reason, it was originally called "Women's Island" (not "Squaw," for that is a [derogatory] word). Over the years, an interesting little encampment was built up on Women's Island, and one canoe was kept at Bomwe Bay for the use of the women. Contrary to what one might expect, this time apart in the women's encampment was greatly anticipated and enjoyed by the ladies. Even at its best, life was difficult for Indian women. This time apart afforded them relief from responsibilities and offered opportunities to rest and refresh themselves. (*Journal of Beaver Island History* 2 [1980]: 39.)

her dowry to his Kitiganing lodge. The villagers were impressed with the dowry, but Pretty Partridge was not impressed with the island, the villagers, nor her new home. Without True Heart to keep it clean and attractive, the lodge had become filthy and dilapidated. Even Ambitious Man's beautifully beaded clothes and moccasins, with which he had cut quite a dashing figure on the mainland, needed mending. The lazy hunter had been eating up the winter's stores. There were skills that Pretty Partridge did not have, nor did she intend to demean herself by acquiring them.

It was not long before the whole village knew that Pretty Partridge was making a fool of Ambitious Man and that she could beat him at his own game of getting someone else to do the work. As the months passed, Ambitious Man lost his braggadocio and became shamefaced. The dowry canoes and the loss of prestige seemed a high price to pay for the presence of Pretty Partridge, who flew his particular nest most of the time anyway. At last, Pretty Partridge disappeared completely in the company of some fishermen from the Lost Lake Village on Pyramid Point, and the shame and degradation of Ambitious Man was complete.

He sat in the ruin of his lodge and ambitious plans and sulked. His emotions ranged between hate for Pretty Partridge, who had made a fool of him, and hate and fear of the spirit of his dead wife, which he imagined to have brought this state of affairs upon him. Not once did it occur to this man that a little hard work on his part might alleviate the situation! There was only one solution, he reasoned, and this was to so placate the spirit of True Heart that she would not continue to visit bad luck upon him. Accordingly, he rummaged among the few remaining belongings of True Heart and found a daintily beaded bag that Pretty Partridge had missed. Of all that remained, this alone was in perfect enough condition to make a spirit offering. Her own handiwork as an offering to her spirit! The incongruity of it was not apparent to the distraught man. As was the custom then, he marked his canoe in black and censed it with cedar, blackened and disheveled his person (which in his state was not TOO much work!), and set out, a sad sight, indeed, intoning petitions to the zhee-be-ug (departed spirits).

On the island where he had once marooned his wife, he set about to peel a cedar tree, as it was traditional to place manidu [spirit] offerings on tall poles. A movement in the underbrush of a nearby swale caught his eye. Immediately the nervous man shot an arrow into the quivering bush. There was a piercing shriek! Ambitious Man dropped his offering and fled, but he did not go far. Heavy guttural sounds pursued him, and he turned to face certain death by a manidu. It was no manidu. It was True Heart, and he knew, from the very human blood that gushed out where his arrow had pierced her abdomen, that she never had become a manidu.

"The child," she gasped piteously, "save your child. . . ."

Ambitious Man remained bowed over the body of True Heart for many hours. He was stunned, fearful, remorseful, penitent, and then—mercifully—inundated with grief.

The coldness of the rising night wind finally roused him to action.

"I shall build her a fine spirit house," he thought, "and then I shall die beside her. I deserve no more." A strange wail that was no coyote cut across his consciousness. In a trance, and still painted with his true wife's blood, Ambitious Man climbed a small rise and saw the rough shape of a bark wigwam. He peered inside. From a pile of rabbit skins, the frightened eyes of a wee boy child looked back at him. Again Ambitious Man was shaken with paroxysms of grief, and this time the quavering voice of the child joined in his wails.

It was a changed Ambitious Man who returned to Kitiganing in the daylight. Dirty and disheveled, he seemed to have no thought for anything but tenderness for the strange child that he carried in his arms. Several women ran to his aid, but he would not surrender the child, nor would he speak until all had gathered in the center of the village around them.

Placing the child before them, he said, "This is my True

Son, the child of my true wife, True Heart." Then he told them all that had happened, sparing himself nothing. Great tears, like no proud Anishinaabe would even allow to form, flowed unbidden down his face as he spoke, washing away the last blood of his truehearted one. The old medicine woman stepped forward and her knowledge verified his story.

"You may beat me to death now," said the grieving Ambitious Man, "but I beg you to raise the True Son of True Heart on Kitiganing in the best Anishinawbimidisiwin [Life in the Fullest Sense]."

Of course the people did not beat Ambitious Man to death. As quickly as they had condemned him before, now they supported him, and they did help him to raise True Son in the finest of the Indian traditions.

As for brave True Heart, she was greatly extolled, and besides the fine spirit house that Ambitious Man had built for her the people raised a big stone cairn. Each woman, every time she went to the island, laid a stone on that monument, with a prayer that she might be as courageous as True Heart. The men also remembered, leaving there, as they passed homeward, the stones with which they had weighted their fishing nets.

When the French traders came, they saw the native people leaving stones and said,

"Why do you do this?"

"It is an offering we make to the spirit of bravery."

"Then we will make one, too," said the traders, "for anyone who paddles these waters surely needs bravery."

By and by the stones were so high that the great cairn could be seen far away across the water. Canoe men and sailors alike used it for a guide. Mothers, climbing the dunes of the nearby islands for kinnikinnick, pointed it out to their children. Fathers, showing their sons how to lay the whitefish nets, waved toward the great cairn.

"Get yourself a woman like True Heart," they would say.

"Enh," the sons would answer, "we shall seek a woman like True Heart."

When the steamers came, they used the stone cairn as a warning to steer clear of the currents that rushed to the reef on the other side. So for another reason, by another race and generation, the memory of True Heart was blessed. In later years, the government built a whole lighthouse of the many stones that had accumulated there [never knowing, of course, their true purpose].

(Journal of Beaver Island History 2 [1980]: 39–43.
Reproduced with permission of the Beaver Island Historical Society)

Cookies and Adders and Otters

It is absolutely astonishing, the manner in which one's mind can give variance to the meaning of memories. I would entitle my becoming-aware years "Cookies and Adders." My parents lived in many different places; we did not always live in the woods. Once in his lifetime, and mine, my father ventured into business. It was a general store, the old-fashioned kind, with everything from shoelaces to chocolate and soap and meat. Whenever a shipment of cookies came in, I would climb on a box, then to the top of the cookie barrel, and just sit there breathing in the delectable fragrance of cookies. Imagine my prestige among contemporaries with a dad who bought and sold cookies!

At this time, we lived in a majestic old Victorian house, which was a relic of lumbering days. It had stood empty for some time, partly because no one seemed to know just how they could manage living in it. But my mother, who remembered clearly her own childhood at Kanglow House in England, knew how to manage it—and manage she did—very elegantly, indeed.

There was a splendid barn–carriage house, under the ramp of which lived a colony of blow [puff] adders. Every shiny day of the summer these blow adders would "take the sun" on this ramp, deploying their bodies rhythmically in geometric patterns.

Encouraged by tales my father told me and pictures in the *National Geographic,* I donned a high-neck jacket, wrapped a towel turban around my head, and played my tin whistle for the adders.

36

Their response was immediate, and we spent many happy hours together. Once Mother came to find me. One look at her child swaying with a bevy of adders and she fell over in a faint.

Not understanding the nature of a faint, I ran for my father, calling, "Come quickly! Mother just died!" The family never let me forget this, and I was annoyed by being teased about this for many years. However, I have many fond memory reflections of my meditations with the adders.

My father's business was a financial disaster. Out there somewhere beyond our lifeways, an undefined monster by the name of "Depression" was beginning to show his monstrous intent. He was abetted by a local agent known as "Bank." Between the two of them, they destroyed our wonderful cookie barrel and adder world and the elegant house that had so delighted my mother. My parents were devastated. The only place left to go was isolated property that long ago had been parceled out to an Indian great-aunt and uncle. We would be safe there forever, as no one else would possibly want such a forsaken location. In order that I should not have to suffer the same shame they felt, my parents arranged to ship me off to relatives for the summer.

[But, as a child,] I was not suffering. The prospect of a long summer with relatives who wore beards and fished from boats and then a return to an exciting new home in the wilderness completely delighted me. Of course, I did not realize then that we would never, ever be able to go back to the elegant house called home again.

Our New Home

[At the close of the summer,] my father met me at the Northport station and brought me to the new place in a wagon drawn by a perspicacious horse named "Old Gray." My, but that trip was an adventure! I leapt from the wagon to hug my pretty mother, who stood anxiously at the cabin door. My father and I unhitched Old Gray, then he put me on his shoulders for a running tour of the barn, the bridge and the brook, the outbuildings, and the animals.

In the snug little kitchen, my mother set out great bowls of steaming squash soup. [That night,] my dad carried me up the steep stairs to the loft bedroom, which was to be all my own.

After prayers, my mama tucked me in and murmured, "Can you be happy here?"

I looked at the high vault of the loft roof, waved back at the pine branch that tapped on the loft window, smelled the fragrance of my new sweet-fern mattress, and said, "Happy? I think this place must be close to heaven."

I was very young then, and I think maybe my response may have been prompted by pleasure in the high loft area that was to be my private living space, but my parents interpreted that answer in quite another way. They laughed, the kind of "laughter medicine" that washes away old bitterness and begins to close the wounds of pride. I sensed the glad relief within it. Suddenly it flashed upon my consciousness that these two grownups really cared very much about what I thought and felt and that my happiness made a portion of their happiness also.

Otter Summer

Zigzagging through our property was a singing creek that ran from the darkness of Unending Swamp into the beach marsh. The portion flowing by our cabin was next to a meadow and was bright and sunny. It always smelled of moistness and mint; its sounds beckoning to exciting discoveries and adventure. I loved that brook but never dreamed of how much I was learning as I shared its glories. It was in that creek that I first saw the otters. I haven't any notion now whether I first saw the otters and had the idea of associating with them because I was lonesome or whether my dad had done such a good job of teaching me about observation in the wilderness.

I just know that at the very beginning of the summer I was going along in that creek, half walking, half wading, just seeing what I could discover, and I heard this merrymaking going on. I stopped, and I thought, "Somebody's having fun." So I moved very slowly and very quietly to the bend in the creek where the clay banks were, and, sure enough, somebody was merrymaking all right.

There were these Nigikog (otters). They had built regular slides, like the ones resorters had in their children's playgrounds, but these were made out of mud—thick, wonderful, ooey-gooey mud, all slippery and shiny. A big mama otter and six little otters were all whizzing down these slides.

When they'd hit the creek water there'd be a big splash and they'd all whistle "Whee-ee-ee!!"

I was simply fascinated. I watched them for a long, long time. They would dive underwater and then surface with that humorous, pleased look on their little whiskered faces. Sometimes there'd be play splashing at each other or their mama. Then they'd crawl out of the water up the side of the bank and whoopee down the slide again. I thought that I surely would like to do that, too. After much time watching them, the desire became more and more irresistible.

Finally, I walked to the head of the first slide, slid down it, hit the water, and said, "Whee!"

The little otters froze to immobility and looked at their mama. And their mama became completely still and looked at me. My father had told me that if one wants to see what some animals are doing one should just stop and become motionless. So there I stood, waist-deep in the brook, perfectly still. The mama otter swam around me, closer and closer, and snuffled at me, all parts of my body. Her whiskers tickled, but I continued to be perfectly still. After maybe twenty minutes of this kind of thing, she shook the water off her body, turned around, and went to the first slide. All the baby otters went after her, and I went right along after them. So the otters and I played slides together all the rest of the summer.

I had such a good time with them. We had more fun! After a while we came to know each other rather well, and certain things were quite easily communicated. One time the mud in one of the slides became cracked clear across and they couldn't mend it with their tails and paws. After I watched for a while, I went and got one of my mother's pans, filled it full of mud, glopped it on the slide, and smoothed it with my hands and the bottom of the pan. The otters were filled with admiration and chattered noisily, coming to pat my hands and put the pan on their heads. They wanted to slide in it, but I feared for our friendship if Mother found her pan banged up. I did feel pleasant over the admiration and wondered to myself if maybe I should become a mud slide builder when I grew up. Just think of all the fun those resort kids with their not-so-sloppy wooden slides were missing. . . .

I suspect my mother thought it was a nice thing I could amuse myself harmlessly at the brook, but she did fuss about my coming home all wet and my clothes quite permeated with mud.

"Well, I can't help it," I said. "What do you want me to do? Take 'em off? The otters don't take theirs off."

My mother replied, "Certainly I don't want you running around the woods naked."

"First of all," I said, "I'm not running around the woods. I'm just going down the slides with the otters—and some other things, but always in the brook and with them along."

My dad gave out with his half-humorous quizzical look. "You know, the town people have special outfits they wear in the water. Why don't you make her something like that out of old clothing?"

After this swimming outfit was made, I could slip in and out of it easily. I wasn't lectured anymore about getting clothes muddy, and everything went along swimmingly. My parents understood about kids splashing in brooks, but I don't think that, just then, they really believed I was going down slides with otters. Probably they thought I was at the age when children have imaginary play friends. They didn't come to investigate, and I was just as glad, especially when Mama Otter began to teach us about catching fish underwater. Every day we became better and better friends and did newer and more interesting things. We walked as far as we could up the brook to the beginning of Unending Swamp. Then I would float, and they would climb on me, so I became a raft, and we would all float together downstream to the place where the slides were.

One day my mother said to me, "I wish you wouldn't go off

and spend all your time in the brook. It's nice to see you so clean, and it is certainly nice for me not to have to bathe you all the time, but why don't you play with your dolls or something like that?"

"Good," I said, "I'll have a tea." I brought out all my dolls and the doll dishes, and then I had this bright idea: I'd invite the otters to tea also. So I asked my mother if I could invite the otters to tea.

"Why, yes," my mother said, "and please give Mrs. Otter my greetings. Tell her I'd appreciate it if she would come also, and we two can have a nice talk while you children are playing." She must have thought she was playing an imaginary game along with me.

Immediately I put on my water outfit and rushed off to the bend in the brook and gave the otters their invitation. I drew it out in the mud that I would not come there but that they were to come to where I burrowed.

They all winked whiskers, nodded heads, and said, "Yeah, yeah, we come."

Of course, I hadn't said to come to tea—that wouldn't mean anything to them. I said, "Come and have something to eat." I even set up a shadow stick so they could tell when to take off for my house.

Such a flurry of activity! I cleaned the dollies and put on their best dresses. Then I washed the doll dishes, little porcelain ones, daintily painted, left over from our days at the big house. Next I wove a long cattail mat to put on the table. Mother looked on benignly, thinking she had initiated a pastime more appropriate to a little girl. She even showed me how to roll the mat corners so they wouldn't unravel. Then I set the doll dishes out, making places for the six little otters, one for me, one for Mrs. Nigik, and one for my mother. Next I made tea, real tea, and put out sugar and cream. I said to Mother, "Please, could I have some fish pieces to serve?"

"I suppose so," she said, "but it will smell."

"Well, otters very much like fish, and if they smell something fishy they won't be offended, they'll be very pleased."

Mother had a pleasant way of saying "ummm-mm-m" when she was half listening. She was still playing along. I don't know what she really thought; I guess maybe she wasn't really thinking.

41

After all, she did have a mountain of matters to keep track of and work on: the house to keep, the meals to prepare, my dad to please (item number one), gardens to plant, tend, and harvest, foods of every season to dry, can, or otherwise preserve, sewing to do—all of which was a very tall order.

I'd asked Mother if I could have some nasturtiums for a small centerpiece—this is what she always did for a tea—and she gave me a little hug to say how pleased she was that I'd noticed. I was doing this when Mother came out the cabin door and saw the otters coming down the path. I stood up to make the proper clicks so Mrs. Nigik would know this being was my mama. Then my mother spoiled it all. She screamed!

Running down the barn path she shrieked, "Wessee, Wessee, there's wild animals invading the front yard."

Father came running. Then he stopped halfway to the house. "It's just her otter friends like she expected." But Mother kept on babbling all sorts of silly things. I remember thinking, "Oh no, how can my mother be so stupid? She had even talked about sitting next to Mrs. Otter." I felt my mother had behaved badly, and I had a hard time convincing the otters that they really were welcome and they were supposed to stay. But when I got the fish pieces out they knew it was really meant for them. They polished off the scrap fish pieces like they were appetizers and consumed the nasturtiums for salad. They even caught on about the tea. I poured the tea, then added cream and sugar, and they drank it with gusto! On the third serving, they didn't bother holding it in their paws—they stuffed everything, little cups and all, into their mouths.

"No, no," I cried, "don't swallow them!"

It was apparent this food wasn't enough for them, so I said, "Come with me. I know a place where there's some more fish." We had a marvelous contraption that had been built across the beach marsh like a boardwalk bridge by my grandfather. It went across that marsh down to the beach where my father had two fish boxes—one where he kept fish that he had caught to keep them alive, and another one where he kept minnows for bait. So I opened the minnow one, and I took them out one at a time, tossing them to the otters. That was wonderful! It was like a circus, with the otters jumping to get the fish, but they became tired of that game after a while, and just jumped into the box where all the minnows were. Of course, that was the place where Father expected to find his minnows when he wanted to go fishing. He often would go running to the beach just before or after a storm because fishing was better then.

They ate all the minnows, every single one. They rubbed their tummies and rolled their eyes and blew fish smells to say what a wonderful party. Then they went off to sleep. But I couldn't go off to sleep; I knew that when my father found his minnow box empty he was going to have a fit. So I went home, and I picked up all the things from the front yard without being told to and slid into my water outfit.

My mother came along and said quite primly, "I think you've spent quite enough time with those otters today."

"I wasn't planning on spending time with the otters."

"Well, why are you dressed up like that then?"

"Well, I was going down to the beach . . . because . . . I . . . well I. . . ." I tried to get out of telling her, but she wouldn't let me, so I had to say what had happened, and that I simply must be allowed to go and refill that box.

"I really don't think you can do that," Mother said.

"I know daddy always does it, but I've watched him many times, so please, please let me try." She could tell I was frightened and very much upset, [so she agreed,] and I *did* refill that box.

All summer I played with those otters, while the little otters grew to be almost as big as their mother. I could always tell them apart; they had different characters, just as people do. We used to rub noses. It was fun. It tickled too. I'd laugh, and they'd laugh. They'd blow bubbles. I was pretty good at it, but I never did become as good as they were.

One day in early autumn we went to the county fair. We came home after two days, and there was a bit of disgruntlement in the atmosphere. I was feeling disgruntled because there were all these wonderful, marvelous, exciting things at the county fair and no one could have any of them unless money was paid. My folks were not going to give me money to buy trash. *I* didn't see them as trash. My mother was a bit disgruntled because she always made things for the county fair and won prizes. That year she had only won six prizes—she usually won nine.

I remember thinking that people were always telling me I should take turns, so I suggested to my mother that maybe she should take turns, too, and let some of the other ladies have prizes that year. That didn't help; in fact, it didn't go over well at all. They just told me I didn't understand what I was talking about.

We arrived at home very late in the evening. Except for occasions like this trip, we hardly ever locked the door. When we opened the screen door to the kitchen, there, between the screen and the wooden door, were seven fish.

My mother started to scold, "Now whoever would be so stupid as to leave fish in the doorway? I suppose now I'll have to scrub the step and scrub the door and it'll smell like fish for days to come. . . ."

I recall my dad was halfway down the barn path to put the horse away. Suddenly he tied the reins to the fence and came racing back down the path to the house.

"Let me see those fish." He looked the fish over very, very carefully, and then he looked at my mother. "Didn't it occur to you while you were doing all this fussing that there is something mighty strange about this happening?"

"It certainly did. From the very beginning I thought this was a very strange situation. And I've told you over and over again. . . ."

"What I'm talking about is this. There is no obvious way these fish got here. There is no obvious way these fish died. Nobody has caught them with a hook. Nobody's speared them. You'll notice there are no holes of any size in them anywhere."

I kept jumping up and down all the time they were discussing. I knew how the fish got there. But they didn't give me a chance to say.

Finally I interrupted, though I had been told never to do that. "I know how they got there."

Lusterware mug that Sadie Cook
used as a centerpiece at tea parties

Mother said, "You do? Did you put them there?"

"No, but I know who did. They're from my otters."

I remember this part so well; it is a little moment light-splintered with joy. My dad didn't show approval very much, but he turned to me like he was seeing me as a person. He gave me a very long and thoroughly approving look, the memory of which warms my heart to this day.

My dad scooped up the fish, and Mother said we must surely throw them away because we didn't know if they were poisonous or not or how long they had been there.

Father said, "No, they're fresh. They're perfectly good. We'll keep them." And the two of them were off on a tiff again. While they were tiffing, I put the fish in a pail of spring cold water and stored it in the springhouse. Next morning I arose from bed very early. My parents thought I'd gone to clean the fish, but I hadn't. I was off to the brook bend. The slides were dry, and the otters weren't there. I went back every day until it got freezing cold and there were skiffs of ice along the edges of the brook. They didn't come back.

Next spring I went back to the bend of the brook and the place of the slides, and then off and on during the summer, but I didn't see them or any mark to show they might have been there. I used to often think that maybe one of them would find a mate and come back to brook bend to live. But they didn't. I kept checking right up until the time that I myself found a mate and went far away to live. I never saw them again.

Incidentally, my father and I ate the fish. My mother wouldn't. The fish were very good, not poisonous, and fresh.

"Think of it this way," Father said, "they left for you the best they could think of. The energy of their gift becomes a part of your body and you forever. It is good." He took another fish.

The otters and I together, we had a splendidly happy summer. They liked peanut butter sandwiches, too.

Early Education

Neighbors as Teachers, Learning about Choices

Mrs. Hinkey

I was maybe four or five. There weren't many other children to play with, and when I wasn't with my animal friends I was often lonely. Maybe Mrs. Hinkey noticed that about me. One morning, I remember, Mrs. Hinkey told me to go ask my mother if I could have coffee with her. I thought that was kind of strange, but I did what she said. My mother said she appreciated her asking and [reminded me not to] eat a lot of cakes or anything like that. I said I wouldn't.

Actually, [Mrs. Hinkey] didn't have coffee. She had Postum.[1] That's what she had every morning. The importance of this occasion, to me, was that this morning I was treated like another adult. The ramifications of choices had never occurred to me before.

Fran Hinkey, my friend, sat at her table with her pot, and she said to me: "Now will you have cream with your Postum? Or will you have sugar? Or will you have cream and sugar? Or will you have cream and double sugar or would you like sugar and double cream? Or would you like it just plain?"

It had never occurred to me that a person had all these choices. In the time of my little life, I had always just accepted what the situation had offered. That this adult considered it important to inquire of *me* what *my* choices were was also very impressive to me.

1. Postum is a coffee substitute made from roasted grains.

So very much was learned from what might be considered a casual acquaintance; eighty years apart we were, generations removed, but we knew that we were friends. She was the lady who taught me how to sing "Silent Night" in German.

And she was the one who said: "It matters not what the countries are, it's where the heart is."

She was one of the roundest, chubbiest women I ever saw, [though short] of stature. She had big hips and a very generous bosom. Not understanding about things such as that, I wondered what she kept in there. And she wore the most beautiful ring. It was a large amethyst set in yellow gold. She'd worn it so long both the ring and the stone had a satin patina.

She used a cane. Her cane was of some wood with a red cast and had a gold handle. I had never seen a cane before.

Sometimes her husband was there, and sometimes he wasn't. It doesn't seem to have been too important to the ongoing of the house. He was a heavy drinker and was often gone for long periods at a time. She couldn't keep track of him. All her children were married and away from home when I knew her.

Mostly we sat on her front porch. It's the only time I ever sat on a front porch. Sometimes Mrs. Hinkey was doing things. But the main thing I remember about Mrs. Hinkey is that she talked to me like I was a grownup.

She would say things like "Do you think I ought to make that? What color would you like? If you could choose, what would you have it be?" Knowing that I couldn't choose . . . she really taught me about choices.

She'd say, "It's nice to know what you'd like if you could have it, because someday, all of a sudden, you're going to find out you can have it, and you shouldn't be lost."

Views on Religion and Spirituality

A lot of the things she told me I've forgotten. Frequently she asked me to read to her because her eyes were very bad. I could read well at a very young age. I could read anything she asked me to read. I could *read* anything, but I often did not understand it. Often it was the Bible, and I could read that because of all the [different] churches I went to. I could read the Bible [in the style of] any church that she wanted. She enjoyed that as much as she enjoyed what was written.

She'd say, "Let's have it 'Free Methodist' style."

She'd point out what she wanted read, and every other word I'd say, "Praise the Lord!" and she'd say, "Yes!"

She talked often about religion. I didn't have any problems with that. Religion was bombarded at me from everywhere. The Christian religion was what she was into. And you see, at that time in my life, I didn't see any difference [between religions]. The thing that bothers people about me is that I still don't.

✳ ✳ ✳ ✳

I find there are some institutions that support certain things that I can't go along with, or they have certain philosophies, defined or undefined, that boggle me. I say it's all right for them, but it's not for me, but I don't think, like some people do, that there's a God here and a God there and that Allah and Buddha and God and the Great Spirit are in little separate compartments someplace, all vying with each other to run the world.

I see no difference if one talks with the Bear Spirits and Guardian Angels, except that the Bear Spirits are a little closer to me because I'm a forest child and because bears are warm beings, I guess. The Bear Spirits have been very good to me, and they have come when I asked them, and angels didn't. I think maybe angels would have come if I had believed in angels, but I believed in the Bear Spirits. I think they're the same kind of thing. I think their manifestation is probably within the person. It doesn't make any difference what you call them. I don't really know, and I don't think it really matters what they are or how they differ from the Great Spirit.

Maybe it's arguable that there are lesser forms of divine spirit there because we can't comprehend any Great Being that is responsible for the whole universe caring about whether we find something we lost or whether we have food or something like that. I don't really think it makes much difference what names are given to them. What's important is that there's a supply of energy there, and by efforts of faith you can reach that energy, and that's what's necessary.

Ispahkwe

Among the memorable characters of my childhood in northern Michigan is an unusual and vital woman by the name of Ispahkwe.

No one seemed to know where she had come from . . . at least she was not blood related to anyone in Onominee . . . but by the time of my memory she was well established in the village social and functional life. In fact, that, in retrospect, seems to be remarkable among a people who were notably clannish.

Ispahkwe had in her possession what seemed to me a veritable storehouse of treasures, among them being a set of fine steel knives, a number of worn but exquisitely executed birchbark scrolls, and a pair of ornate silver earrings that she wore constantly. These were the first silver work I ever saw . . . and we children were not the only ones who found them, and Ispahkwe, attractive. Those earrings danced in the sunlight as Ispahkwe swung up the trail with her water pails. When she sang or danced with the rest of us at the village gathering place, they caught the rosy gleam of the firelight. Even in the comparative gloom of her little cabin, they seemed to possess an animation of their own.

Just as the burnish of the earrings disseminated reflected light, so did the personality of Ispahkwe play and reflect upon the people of the village. Although I did not realize it then, this was strange, for in those days few women lived solitary lives, and those who did were in that position for some unpleasant reason—often the suspicion of witchcraft.

However, people did come from all over to get her to cut

50

birchbark for them. Most people would cut it, clean it, and sand it smooth, then leave it under something to flatten it out, but when Ispahkwe cut it, it often was immediately ready for use. She would find a tree with just the right size and shape of the piece needed, then deftly cut through the outer bark, never touching the cambium layer, which would hurt the tree, and the piece of bark would pop right off, ready to use. She could even do this with pieces large enough for canoes.

One day, on her way from the spring through the village, while walking past a group of women sitting on logs set around a cleared place in the middle of the village and quilting, Ispahkwe heard them gossiping.

She stopped, and said in the middle of one woman's story, "Maybe that's so and maybe it isn't. Unless you absolutely know that it is true, you shouldn't say anything, because it could ruin that woman's reputation."

The women didn't really agree with her, so Ispahkwe continued, "She has enough trouble already. She doesn't need you to add to it. Don't let me hear of you doing this again." Then she walked on.

When she reached the edge of the clearing, Ispahkwe looked back. It was plain to her that they were continuing to gossip. So she put her buckets down, and, faster than anyone could see, Ispahkwe's knife whipped through the air and landed with a "thunk" in the middle of the quilt that they were working on. (The piece thus pierced later had to be covered with a new appliqué.) She walked back to the women, retrieved her knife, and said, "Don't let me hear of you doing this again. It is not just sharp knives that can kill." Then she walked back to her buckets, picked them up, and continued on to her lodge.

When the time eventually came for Ispahkwe's departure from this cycle, there was a great buzz among the villagers as to what should become of the beautiful silver earrings. All her other possessions (with the notable exception of the birchbark scrolls) Ispahkwe had willed away in the best Anishinaabeg tradition.[2]

2. Birchbark scrolls are used by Native teachers as teaching tools and memory aids. As birchbark can last for centuries, these scrolls are treasured family and tribal heirlooms.

On the day of the ritual burial, underground swells of discussion about the earrings had reached monumental proportions. There was not a man, woman, or child in the village who had not, at some time and for some reason, coveted the earrings. Wise old Chief Payaheena, who was himself close to the end of his Sun Trail, made the concern public.

"If I should remove the silver earrings from the body of our friend," he spoke out, "who would wear them?"

Some looked at the chief and then looked away. Some looked at each other . . . and looked away. Some looked at the earrings, and their eyes fell. No one spoke. Two faraway birds called in the stillness.

"Then we have the answer," said Payaheena, "let no one discuss it again."

So the beautiful silver earrings were buried with the beautiful woman for whom they were made, and nobody ever knew the source of either. Ispahkwe also had a beautiful song, which had been given her by her mother at birth.

And when the people asked her if they could continue to sing it after she was gone she said yes.

ISPAHKWE'S NIGHT WIND SONG

I am sad and lonely—
I call on the nightwind,
    Mother—
    Father—
       Come!
Hark I hear an answer:
The aspens are talking,
The waters are laughing,
"We are your parents:
You are our child."
    The aspens my mother?
    The waters my father?
    If you are my parents

Then come to me—
Now.
Nobody . . .
comes.
I am sad and lonely—
Could there be a lover?
I cry on the night wind.
Somebody . . .
Come

✻ ✻ ✻ ✻

One of the Anishinaabeg customs related to Westing (passing over) has been the source of the white man's term *Indian Giver*. Traditionally, whenever an elder might feel his last step toward the West imminent, he invites friends, neighbors, and relatives to a giveaway feast. At this time, the host brings out of his dwelling every single material thing he owns and presents them to the persons he wishes to have them in the future. At the conclusion of the feast, the same items are carried back into the dwelling and left there by the recipients to be used by the donor until the time of his completed Westing. White people, observing this peculiar ritual, did not understand that it is a type of public will executed while the owner is still able to delineate his wishes clearly. In this way, family and clan disputes over valued possessions are eliminated. The white people saw only that some stupid Indian had given away the things he owned at a time when they are still needed and that the equally stupid recipients had turned right around and given their valuable gifts back again! Thus began the term *Indian Giver,* meaning a person who gives something and then takes the use of it back again.

(From Direction We Know: Walk in Honor, *by Keewaydinoquay, copyright MKD 1979)*

Names

"Nishnaabe," "nishnaabe" . . . some slang might refer to "nishnaabs" . . . a bunch of "nishnaabs." One particular time we were playing a game, and I don't know who used this word indirectly, but we had a really hot game going and he [an elder] made us all stop and come over and sit down around him and he took a long time there to explain to us that we don't use *nishnaab* or *nishnaabe* ... that the proper word is *Anishinaabe.* He told us that we must say it the right way and not make any exception to it, because the other way was vulgar and crude and made it seem as if we couldn't keep the dignity of the People. I remember that one so strongly because I was one of the ones who was getting real exercised about playing. I was very anxious to win. Then afterward we felt sort of intimidated about it.

$$* \;\; * \;\; * \;\; *$$

I was not taken away to a boarding school like so many Indian children.[3] Two or three times somebody came to try to find me, but they came back to the schoolteacher and said, "There's nobody out there." I didn't know it, but my folks had a permit from the state to teach me at home. I knew other kids had been taken away, but they made it sound like a real privilege, so I was kind of disappointed. It seemed kind of exciting, to be taken away to a foreign place.

When I was older, after I was apprenticed to Nodjimahkwe in older childhood, there were very few kids left around here. I'm sure, not to take away that they were kind to me as a person, but I'm sure that was a reason why so many of the elders reached out to me and said so many nice things and were indulgent.

I experienced such joy from hearing stories when I was young. At the time, I did not realize how generous were these gifts I was receiving, but, over the years of my life, often what I heard as a child came leaping into consciousness to serve as guide and support in trying to walk a life of balance and honor.

3. Indian boarding schools were once found throughout the United States. They were established under a federal program with the goal of conquering Native American populations by denying Native children the right to speak their own languages. Instead they were forced to speak only English and to abandon their own customs and cultures.

My parents taught me to respect elders, and it was a great joy to me, for I loved hearing the stories they had to share. I spent a great deal of time with some, and heard about life and the way things used to be. I begged for stories, and sometimes it was hard to tell who garnered more pleasure from this sharing.

I was able to help elders with jobs just right for small hands and fast legs, even though I did not always understand why they couldn't do it themselves. But what the elders gave me served me for a lifetime, and I sometimes wonder if the elders might have had something to do with me not being forced to go to Indian boarding school. It could be. At that time, I only knew how much joy these relationships brought to me, even though I took it for granted at the time.

The Ettawahgeeshiks

The Ettawahgeeshiks were an elderly couple who lived in a small house that they kept spotlessly clean. They always were glad when I came and offered me cookies and something to drink.

The Ettawahgeeshiks were some of the few adults who asked me a lot of questions about myself and how my life was going. They were clearly interested in what I thought and felt and experienced. I'd like to say to older people, who may think that they cannot make a difference, that this is a time when you can really reach out and have something worthwhile to offer to young people. It isn't unusual for a child to carry the unobligated kindness of an adult in her heart for a lifetime.

The Ettawahgeeshiks always made me feel welcome. If they could, they would stop whatever they were doing to spend time with me. And if they couldn't they would carefully explain why and then ask for my help. They were, by then, old and physically handicapped, so both heavy work and work requiring a delicate touch sometimes was very difficult for them. Once they were straining to transplant a tiny tree and I was able to help get it in its hole. Another time, I was able to help Mrs. Ettawahgeeshik with some dyeing. I really liked that because my mother dyed many things but usually wouldn't let me help.

The Ettawahgeeshiks didn't teach me how to make choices, like Mrs. Hinkey did, but they did show me how to enjoy life, no matter how limited choices become. They also impressed me with their closeness. Even as a little girl, I could see how much they depended on and helped each other.

But to me, at my young age, the most important thing about the Ettawahgeeshiks was that they had the most beautiful, old-style ceremonial outfits that I had ever seen! These outfits were incredible! I've seen other hand-done work like these outfits in museums since, and I may have met others who owned such valuable heirlooms, but no one had ever let me see and even hold them before.

The Ettawahgeeshiks, on the other hand, not only had the most exquisitely worked outfits I could ever imagine, even more amazingly, anytime I wanted to see them they would get them out and show them to me!

Besides the beauty of their beadwork, these his-and-hers outfits matched, which was not usually done in those days. The Ettawahgeeshiks' outfits were done in wild-rose and oak-leaf patterns, and they were just exquisite. Mr. Ettawahgeeshik's outfit had leggings, a vest, armbands and gloves, all with an oak-leaf pattern. Mrs. Ettawahgeeshik's outfit was done in a wild-rose pattern.

The roses were done in delicate shades of old rose. The pointed red-oak leaves were done in reds and muted oranges, and the rounded white-oak leaves were beaded in tans and yellows with accents of orange. It seemed like an odd combination until Mrs. Ettawahgeeshik explained that the oak leaves and roses were to show that in everything that lives there is the need for both strength and gentleness.

Thanks to the Ettawahgeeshiks I knew from a young age what really beautiful Indian regalia looked like. Some people didn't believe me when I described it to them, thinking that I was only a white schoolteacher who couldn't know what I was talking about. And I probably wouldn't have known, either, if this couple hadn't been so generous with their time and their kindness. Back when I was a teacher, few people had regalia this fine. Most of the gatherings by then were weddings and funerals rather than powwows.

I realize now how hard it might have been for these elderly people to go up in the loft and bring down their outfits, both because of having to climb and because I was just a grubby little girl. But they never said no if they could help it. And they never acted "put out" by my visits.

My mother wouldn't let me call them Grandfather and Grandmother. She didn't think it was respectful due to her English upbringing. I called many persons Aunt and Uncle, but the Ettawahgeeshiks were always called Mr. and Mrs. Ettawahgeeshik. When we moved away from there, I never saw them again, but they forever will have an enshrinement in my memory.

More about Our New House in the Woods

The place where we lived was a log cabin—one great big room. On one end of it was a huge fireplace that was so big! On the other end of the room my parents had their bed, some chests, and a little stairway to my loft. When I was in my loft I could look down and see everything that was in the room except what was directly beneath me. Off the main room was a lean-to kitchen, but it wasn't like a lot of lean-tos, not shacky. It had a nice big range and a fireplace that was always kept smoldering slightly. That range was our heat source for the winter.

That was a very nice vantage place, that loft. That's where I looked down from when I first saw Pearse with little Val fox in his mackinaw and he motioned my folks to come out into the kitchen.[4] I used to think it would be the nicest thing in the world to be a grownup and stay up half the night and have wonderful things to

4. A mackinaw is a heavy waterproof jacket.

57

eat and talk about things that children couldn't hear. I didn't realize they were really working.

The Story of Val

I will never forget the Winter of Screaming Trees. We heard it said there would be a heavy winter, but just how heavy no one realized.

That winter some great learnings came into my life. It is the first time I remember having been thoroughly frightened. I learned about fear. I learned stories and teachings from some elders who were not with us the following winter. So I learned the value of continuity. I came to the understanding that I was as important a unit of the family as any other. And I experienced the presence of little Val, who became so much a part of my heart that he has never left.

The snows came early, which wasn't unusual, but they never seemed to stop, which was unusual. By December, the [amount of] snow became a cause for alarm. My father had put up extra attempts at insulation for [our] animals and extra snow barriers for the necessary traveling paths for the people. He still spent a good half of the day at snow removal. My mother used to laugh and say, "Oh, your father is out there rearranging the snow again." But there was a fearful edge to her laughter.

The log cabin where we lived was one great long room, two stories high. At the south end rose a fireplace so gigantic that it almost composed the entire south wall except for the windows. The window frames had been steam bent and at one time were filled in with translucent rawhide. The hearth stretched across the front to make a long stone bench. Back in the throat of the fireplace were sooty shelves where, on low-fire days, my mother kept bricks to warm for nighttime cold toes and big brown pots of beans and thrumity, "creeing" [slow cooking] for the meals of a fortnight ahead. [Freezing weather helped keep the cooked food from spoiling.]

On the north side of the cabin house was my own private loft, with a darling little diamond-shaped window that looked right out into the treetops, a personal screen eye through which I could watch activities in season. Under the loft was my parents' room, which consisted of a built-in closet, a dresser, a highboy, and a goose-feather bed my mother had made before her marriage. A little stairway led up to my loft. It was a wonderful vantage point, that loft, which became alternately, under the magic of my imagination, an open sesame to dreamland, a warm cocoon, a cool treetop dwelling, or a marvelous machine to travel to lands afar. I could observe everything that happened down below—except occurrences and conversations in the lean-to kitchen. There the great range winked fiery warmth at us all and Mother worked her gustatory enchantments with pots and kettles.

One morning in that out-of-season winter, we awakened to find that the entire house was snowed in tight. We'd already seen the snowbanks insulate us to the tops of the windows. But now even Father's great strength could not open the front door nor the kitchen door! After many trials and discussions, it was decided that I should be put out through the little loft window to make my way [through the snow] to the outside of the kitchen door. Fortunately, the tools were already there [leaning against the outside of the cabin].

All at once, I was the focal point of hope, the possible savior of the family; every concern of all kinds was directed toward me. Big Father could not go through the loft window, even medium-sized Mother could not strain through. Mother mourned that I might sink and freeze or suffocate in the snow. Father kept reassuring her that there was much oxygen in the snow and that I would be all right, just so long as I kept "swimming" [through the drifts].

I was not afraid at all; in fact, I recall clearly an absolute feeling of exaltation as I flew from the loft window into the soft white ocean and propelled [myself] easily in the direction of the kitchen door. Chiseling the snow-ice from the door cracks was the hardest part, but even that was not difficult. As soon as I had the ice chiseled out, Father bent his strength against the door from the inside.

A glacial wall and I fell together into the kitchen. I was a hero. I had accomplished something in my own right. Gravely, I shook hands with my parents. None of that hugs and kisses stuff.

Suddenly, as suddenly as the heavy snow had begun to fall that year, the weather began to thaw. In some places, the groundcover completely disappeared. The sap began to rise in the trees. A thaw . . . in late January? Unheard of! To people who live close to Earth, this seemed a portentous sign indeed, but what did it portend? Almost every person had his own idea. The young people began to prepare their waders and anxiously scout the fish ladders in nearby streams.

The older women covered the skeletons of the work wigwams and industriously began making the rough birchbark mukukuk [buckets] that capture maple syrup. Traveling to school was out of the question. Huddled in the work wigwams, the Grand Elders began to recite stories and legends, to sing some of the working songs seldom heard, and to sketch some of the hieroglyphs and decorative signs that had fallen into disuse.

I was entranced. Only Mother complained that I forsook my work at home and scampered off to the work wigwam. She was right. I would do anything to absorb these old-new learnings. I floated on an ecstatic cloud of desire. Salutations to the spirit of Nagowikwe (Sand Woman), who told me so many stories!

One evening during that long winter thaw, I stood at the loft rail in my flannel nightie singing blessings to my parents, who stood on the hearth below. All at once there was a thunder of complicated noises at the outside kitchen door. I looked up to see Pearse Quirck, our neighbor of some three miles away, who appeared for all the world like a gigantic outsized bear in his winter fur, dripping slushy snow all over Mama's clean floor. He made motions for my parents to come quickly into the kitchen.

It was not particularly surprising to have Pearse show up at our house unannounced. He was a giant of a man who gave out that he was the last of the voyageurs and got away with it. He spoke poor English, good French, and fluent Ojibway, and he lived alone in an efficient little house, where his wife and child were buried in the flower garden. Pearse had been a part of the local environment ever since I could remember, and I took him for granted, like the trees.

How I did long, that particular night, to be able to see through the cabin wall into the kitchen! But I knew better than to beg. I could hear the rise and fall of voices, the clink of cups and muffled adult laughter, but this was not for me, so I crept stoically between the covers. It was difficult being a child, I often thought then.

Next morning at my customary breakfast table place there was a basket. On the handle was a red heart torn out from a magazine page, and imprinted thereon were these words: "TO OUR VALENTINE." The basket was filled with "hay" from last Easter, but something new had been added: the fragile green strands rose up and down rhythmically, and when I moved them aside—there was a beautiful, colorful, miniature kit fox, perfect in every detail. I was beside myself with delight, and I promptly named him "Val" because he had come on Valentine's Day.

This was the secret that Pearse had nestled in his mackinaw the night before. He'd not been sure my parents would approve of such a pet for me. Pearse ran a trapline through our property, and he had come upon a female fox with her legs broken in the trap. He could tell by her full dugs that she had young somewhere—no doubt betrayed into an early delivery much as the great thaw had fooled the trees and the plants. So he looked around and soon found the den with several frozen kits. But at the bottom was this one robust kit, which he gathered immediately into the warmth of his mackinaw.

I was so happy with Val I'd willingly have licked his glossy fur as his mama would have done, but my parents took a dim view of this. Mother brought out a little hand-knit blanket and a baby brush and comb set that she had sentimentally saved. Father devised a thin rawhide "bottle" in which I warmed diluted milk, either in my hands or against my body. Nobody but Val and I expected him to survive, but he did, and we bonded immediately.

There was a strange aftermath to the great thaw—one that involved the presence of fear, as I have mentioned. The sap had arisen in the trunks of some trees and then coursed down the main branches. When winter returned and the woodlands froze again, the frozen sap broke open the bark in thin places and formed delicious icicles. The sap of different trees made different-tasting icicles, and in the winter sunlight I loved wandering the woods and tasting the flavors offered by various trees.

The freezing evening, however, was another story. Branches began to hiss and sigh loudly and then broke open with screams. Even worse were the night deaths of whole trees. As the trunks split open, there was a series of sharp reports, which echoed throughout the woodland, followed by the piercing death agony call as a tree heart quite literally burst apart. These were my old friends: my swing tree, my jungle rope tree, my sweet-treat tree, my basket tree, etc., calling to me for help I could not give.

Mama and Daddy kept trying to console me, but they had never heard anything like it either.

"Not the walnut," my father would say, "please not the walnut."

"Not the yellow plum," said Mother, "I didn't preserve enough this year." But I had both seen and tasted the icicles on the yellow plum, and I knew. She was a dainty arbor, that yellow plum, and her farewell was high and thin and sweetly sorrowful, as befitted a dainty yellow plum.

"There goes the yellow jam tree," I said, and I cried.

Mother was frightened. She didn't really believe that bit about trees having spirits, but Daddy moved up and put his hand on my shoulder. He knew also that it was the spirit of the yellow jam tree that had soared out into the cold starry night, for his own special Earth Spirits were the trees, and he loved them deeply. I cuddled against Mama and Daddy, and reached out and cuddled Val, and together we tried to endure the passing of so many friends and relatives. Certainly I don't wish you such an experience, but you should know that it IS possible for such a winter to be.

The springtime of my seventh or eighth year found Val following at my heels like a well-trained puppy, only much more beau-

Maple sapcicles

tiful; he was always slender and sleek and brightly colored. I hadn't ever been taught about animal training, but I certainly did the best job I could at that for Val. He'd been tolerated as an inside pet only because it was so bitter cold, and I didn't intend for him to be considered as anything but my companion, inside and out. He learned to eat from a bowl and not leave scraps on the floor; he learned to catch the water from the outside spigot in his mouth but not put his mouth upon it. During the winter, Val had used a box in the woodshed, but now Daddy told me to take him to the woods, dig a hole, and show him how to use it. He never had to be shown anything more than that once. It was hard to believe exactly how smart and intelligent he was.

Val ran at my heels in the early spring—but he ran ahead of me forever afterward—across the meadows, up the ripply sand dunes, down the beaches. He always circled back to nudge me toward something he had found or to investigate with me something I had found. People remarked how pleasant it was to see "that little girl and her dog exploring the wild places," and "what a lovely color," they'd say, . . . and "what breed did you say he was?"

My father, anticipating some racial slurs (of which there were heap plenty in those days) turned aside and muttered under his breath—"both RED."

Mother, as a result of her British social training, would just bob pleasantly and say something like, "Oh, sort of a foxhound, I do believe. A nice mutt for the child, anyway. You know how it is with dogs." She had turned an incipient undercurrent aside.

Val's accomplishments as a "gofer" were astonishing. Previously that had been my job, but Val outshone my poor efforts. He would be out of the storage house and back with the desired object before I'd barely started. He never did learn to speak the American language, but there was no doubt whatsoever of his understanding. Sometimes he would make a mistake, such as the time Mother mentioned a trowel and he came back with a towel. These happenings would send us into paroxysms of laughter. Such fun!

We had a wonderful springhouse-cum-refrigerator, which had been engineered by Grandfather. A circular stone wall was built around the emergence of a small but reliable cold-water spring. Mounted on this was a wooden cover with an iron ring. This, when lifted back, revealed octagonal cedar shelving where eggs and milk and leftovers could be kept. If Mother should just mention something from that spring house, Val would be off like an arrow down the springhouse path. When I arrived he would be sitting on the springhouse cover, his eyes crinkling with merriment and his tongue lolling out with foxy laughter, as if to say, "Where have you been all this time?"

He would even help carry small packages appropriately wrapped—such as eggs in a basket—without mishap. Often people would say, "I don't know as you can trust that animal with food." We'd wondered about that ourselves sometimes, but we always fed him so well, and he had such a desire to please, that there were fewer mishaps with Val than there were with me. Except once.

A minister from the nearest town came to dinner. Mother had made out he was coming for the pleasure of a discussion with an educated man like my father, but it did turn out he came for the reasons you'd expect when a minister came to call—good food. While the grownups were having a predinner sample of elderberry wine, Mother had left the roasted chicken in the serving dish to keep warm on the range door. I came around the corner just in time to see the roast chicken (with a tail remarkably like Val's) moving on little fox feet toward the backyard door! While Mother rescued the roast, Father rolled up a newspaper and spanked Val noisily. After that, whenever Val showed any signs of undesirable behavior, all we had to do was roll up a newspaper.

Hunters began to report a fantastic big red fox on our land. Of course, the only ones that should have been hunting there were Pearse and ourselves, and Pearse would never draw a gun on Val. But many folks did not pay attention to woodland regulations, especially if it was Indian land. Father and Pearse devised a heavy leather collar for Val, giving his name and explaining that he was a pet. This satisfied me but not the two men. I know now that they were as concerned for me as for Val.

The local postman who drove our rural route each week took to carrying a shotgun, as his wife wanted a fox collar to wear to church and Val's fur was purported to be super gorgeous. Also there was a remarkable distinguishing feature: just before the usual markings of a fox tail, Val had a thin band of pale yellow hair, actually giving his whole tail a luminous quality. Father tried talking to this man, who had always been a friendly mail person, and even had me parade Val so he'd recognize him, never dreaming the man would persist in hunting a little girl's pet.

I told the mailman, "Jesus wouldn't want to see Val dead on her shoulders," but that didn't seem to make any difference either. It was stylish at that time for ladies to wear a fur piece.

There was another problem regarding Val, although it was mostly my father who was concerned about it. Father took me aside and explained about how all species seek their own kind for mates and this was a right and good thing for the Balance of the Earth and all its Kindred.

"Yes," I said, "I've known about that for some years now." (I learned to understand about sex in that loft. Field mice lived in my mattress. I was so intrigued watching them that I didn't tell my parents about them until there was a whole family of babies and I had field mice droppings in all my clothes. My parents thought at first it was lice and were very concerned. Finally, I had to tell them there were field mice in my mattress. After Val slept with me in the loft, there were no more field mice. I think that's the only reason my mother tolerated him there.)

Father gulped and answered, "Yes, well now—just so. One of these moonlit nights, when the foxes are dancing and calling across the swamp, Val will just slip off and go to them so there can be more little foxes with yellow rings on their tails. He will be happier there with his own little fox mate and his own little foxes, and that is what we want for him, isn't it?" Now, I know very well that he was trying to make me feel good about something he thought was about to happen, that I was supposed to agree with him and begin to be glad about Val's going away. But NO, I didn't want that to happen.

Val wouldn't be happier somewhere else without me, and I knew that for sure. It turned out I was right. Val would go away some nights, but he always came back the next day.

"Well, I'll be damned," said Father.

"Talk like that and you probably will be," said Mother. And that ended the concern about Val's sex life and the call of the wild.

It did not end the concern about my attachment, nor the concern for Val's life at the hands of some hunter. In those days, the state sent out rangers once a year, dropping them by parachute over the length of the islands to clean out and restore the fire lanes in the forests there. Then in a week they would send a boat up the chain of islands to pick up these fire rangers. The last stop of these workers was with a single-prop plane in the great meadow beside Cat Head's largest sand dune. Again Mother made out that they stopped with us because of my father's education and that he was able to talk with them so intelligently about their work. Now, I reason, it was much more likely that it was the last chance to eat an elegant meal like my mother prepared and to obtain homemade delicacies to augment their "army issue" diet.

Anyway, my parents thought if they could talk these rangers into taking Val with them my tender heart could be saved from a forever-type sorrow and they would never let me take a wildling for companion again. Mother devised a sturdy gunnysack traveling bag, and Daddy and Pearse made leather neck straps so the parachuter's hands would be free. It had come to the place where the choice was to love a dead Val near me or love a live Val somewhere on the uninhabited islands. Not much of a choice. Life without Val presented a dismal aspect.

The day of departure was a bad dream. I don't remember much of it except the actual departure. When they tied the bag over Val's face I thought I would die.

"Not to worry," called the nice young ranger over the infernal noise of the engine. "He's probably the first fox in all history to drop in a parachute."

That comment was meant to be funny and compassionate, but humor and compassion are not always successful bandages when your heart is bleeding. I ran at full tilt across the meadow and up the sand dune. I wanted to be sure to see the first fox in history make his parachute jump. Far away above the great cliffs of South Fox Island a black dot disengaged from the plane. Oh, Val. As I turned from the island panorama I was sobbing so copiously I could see nothing, so I thought. One of the dune-top conifers suddenly split, seemed to hesitate in the air, and then took off southward with massive running steps. Pearse—he and the conifer tree—had been watching all the time. It was soon after that Pearse convinced my parents to let me go on my vision quest. He knew that I was still trying to belong.

Every late summer when the rangers came back from the islands I was there to meet them.

"Had they seen Val? How was he now?"

"Oh, yes," they'd seen Val. A large fox had come and slept by their campfire the first night. When they tossed tidbits, he stood on his hind legs to catch them and never missed.

Two years later a survey crew told me they'd been surrounded by little foxes with yellow rings on their tails. Hundreds of them!

They tapped the map where the shapes of the islands showed. It read: North and South *Fox* Islands.

$$* \quad * \quad * \quad *$$

I learned to read out of the *National Geographic.*

My father would say, "Find all the words with *a* on the page." Then I would find all the *thes* . . . the *s* and the *ands*. My mother didn't think that was quite the way it should be done, but I knew how to read before I ever went to school.

I went to school at Northport [intermittently]. I rode our horse, Old Gray. And I had a very good attendance record as long as we had Old Gray, even though the teacher never liked me very much. She didn't like it that I got good grades. . . . I don't know why she didn't like that. I know when we first started to read, I remember the first page said, "See Spot run." She went around the class and had everybody read it, and they'd get a gold star if they got it right. When she got to me, I turned to the last page of the book and I read that right. I thought she'd give me three gold stars, but she made me stand in the corner and made me hold up my hands in front of me. Every time they'd start to fall down, she'd crack them with a ruler. I had to be a teacher myself before I could understand anything about that at all. I guess she thought I was being a smart aleck. But I had imagined those gold stars.

That was the beginning of her not liking me too well. It never changed, and she was the teacher through eighth grade. She had her own home and her own problems and also the problems with the Indians [because] the whole town of Northport [had] just [been] taken away from the Indians.[5] There were a lot of [unpleas-

5. The Odawa and Ojibway of Northport had been forced off of the land allotted to them by treaties due to bureaucratic mismanagement and fraudulent land dealing. At the time of Keewaydinoquay's intermittent schooling near Northport, Native people were trying to find a way to keep from being evicted from their rightful holdings. This scenario was enacted time and time again all over Michigan and the entire United States. Among the papers at the Holy Hill Center is a document that refers to one of Keewaydinoquay's ancestors, Isaac Blackman, also known as Mukdaahena. In it, he is trying to resecure land that had been promised under the *Treaty of 1855.*

ant] ramifications that I didn't know as a child. At school this bothered me [as well as my teacher].

I got so I could read better than anyone else. But I didn't brag about it. My parents carefully explained to me that I should never make it seem like I could do things better than anybody else.

"But," I said, "I do."

"Yes," they said, "but you shouldn't make it seem like that, lest it should hurt the feelings of the other people. Just don't say anything. Just stand there quietly, and if you are really good at it you'll get picked for that." But I never got picked to be Pocahontas for our Thanksgiving play. They always dressed me up like a Pilgrim. And I wanted to be Pocahontas!

I may have held my tongue, but I could still use my fists. Boys would pick on me at school and call me names . . . "Indian" . . . depending on who was talking. As long as I rode Old Gray, my parents weren't worried about me—because I could swing up and I'd be off and away and no one could catch me. But when Old Gray died they were most concerned. They never said it, but they must have known [that he could keep me safe]. Old Gray was the kind of horse that wouldn't go across ice unless it was firm.

My route to and from school every day took me and Old Gray along the north side of Kehl Lake. My mother didn't really like me going this way because of the Wabeno burial [site].[6] She was always afraid that I would see things that she felt weren't appropriate for a young lady.

Choices

The fact is, I carry psychological wounds from my parents that were unintentional. They trusted Old Gray, but they didn't trust me—despite all the things they had taught me. My Dad had taught me how to walk in muck so you wouldn't sink. If there weren't logs or trees, you'd walk with a bunch of brush under your arm and

6. Wabeno is a spiritual practice of Anishinaabeg people. It translates as "People of the Dawn."

throw them out ahead. They never seemed to think I learned any of that.

Actually, I did endanger my life so many times I can't imagine how I grew up. When I think of some of the things that I did myself . . . a lot of them I never told my parents about. I thought, well, maybe when I get older . . . those things alone would make a book, but it wouldn't be good for children to read. . . .

When I was about four years old, I went out to the wood pile to bring in some logs. The pile was stacked somewhat precariously, and when I pulled on one log, they all started to fall in on me, so I couldn't move. I think it was one of the dogs that found me.

I can remember one time when I was sunk in the swamp up to here. I knew what to do, and I did it. You grab onto the nearest thing that will float and try to float yourself. But sometimes when you're pulled down you can't, you know. I grabbed onto the nearest stump and tried to pull myself out, and it became apparent that I was not going to be able to "pull me out," and pull my overshoes out, too. I had those old-fashioned black overshoes that have the black latches—metal things—and they were new ones, too. I tried and tried. Finally, I just had to make a choice. I realized I was not going to get out with the overshoes. It was pretty bad because I had to walk all the way home without them.

My mother went to school to look at the leftover overshoes in the schoolhouse and talk to the teacher. A lot of money had been spent on those new overshoes. I never confessed a thing because I knew that if I ever told them what had happened they'd never let me go into the bog again, and that was the only way in those days, I had to make any money [I needed] for myself. I used to collect specimens and take them to the university. I suspect that maybe that also had something to do with the way things turned out . . . my lifelong interest in plants.

Myxomycetes Story

When I was what was considered then an "in-between-girl," between child and adult, I did a lot of running and was real fast. I

70

could also catch fish with my hands. Well, my mother was having company and she didn't have anything stashed away that was good enough, so she told me to catch some fish, some fresh trout. Under ordinary circumstances, I would have welcomed this opportunity to get away from camp.

There was a big log that ran across the river—actually a fast-flowing creek. But there was something on it, just where I usually lay, very very still, until I saw a fish and scooped it up and threw it flip-flop on the bank, and the others would never know where it went.

The other fish would just look at each other and say, "Where did Bill go?"

But there was something there. It looked like somebody's spit, or half vomit. There were little white puffy things around the edges. I sure wasn't going to lie down in it and catch fish. So I went to three or four other places but had no luck. Finally I decided I would have to go back there and make some kind of mattress and lie down where that awful stuff was. I went back and . . . it had moved!

So I got my fish, but what really blew me away was that this gooey mass had moved two or three feet, so by the time I got back I could lie down without getting into it. I couldn't wait to tell my folks about this thing on the log [though when I did, there was a very strange reaction].

"Well," my grandfather said, "there will be no liars in this family." Until I could stand up and acknowledge I was lying, I would be banished to the back—the little wigwam out back— with no food.

I had it on the tip of my tongue to say, "But I bet you'll all take my fish and eat 'em." But I didn't because that wasn't the thing to do in those days. You always showed respect to your elders. So that's what happened. I *was* hungry that night . . . let alone the next day. Finally the next day, still mad, I thought surely my mother would come to see me and explain something to me, but she didn't. So the fourth day I said I had something to say.

Everyone was together, and I was invited to come, and I said, "I'm sorry about what I said about the thing in the forest."

Everybody waited, and I waited, and finally my grandfather said, "Get Zhatay[7] a bowl of soup." But I never said I didn't see it [that would have been the real lie].

Many years later, when I went back to high school, they had a biology department, and the first thing I did was to go there and ask if there was some kind of plant or animal that looked like this. In those days, most people just went through eighth grade. The person who taught biology was a literature major, but she had some biology so she taught it. She said there was no such thing. All that time I was looking for some way to justify my truth telling. I knew I'd seen it. I knew it was there! [Then] when I first went to college and found a real biology department, they knew right away what I was talking about: Myxomycetes.

Later I got into trouble for teaching something similar. I was called in about some "wild sex stories."

I said, "I can't very well teach biology without talking about reproduction."

They said, "The idea of a plant or animal that is male and female and neuter and all three of them can produce on their own? That's against God's holy word!"

God forgot to tell the Myxomycetes.

7. Zhatay was a nickname of the young Keewaydinoquay.

More Education
and Schooling

The Drum and Me

Where we lived when I was a young girl, if you climbed the dunes and then cut across the woods you looked right at North Fox Island and could see South Fox clearly, and on really clear days you could see the rest of the islands. When I was seven or eight, I remember that we took the canoe from Cat Head Bay to South Fox, South Fox to North Fox, North Fox to Amik Island, and on up the shore of Amik and across to Kitiganing Island. We landed over at Pete Manidu's because he was a shirttail relative of ours and a member of the clan we belonged to.

Pete Manidu was an Indian man. I wouldn't call him a settler because when people say settlers they usually mean some white person who came in and took up land. I don't know the exact lineage, but our family was intermarried with the Manidus. His parents would have been among the Indians that were given tracts of land on Kitiganing Island by the federal government. I remember my dad describing Pete Manidu as a "misplaced genius" because he could do just about anything. He had his little place all fixed up. He made a large boat for fishing, and he had sawed, cut, planed, and steamed all the wood to shape into his boat. That boat was driven ashore by a storm after he died, and it sat there at the end of Manidu Bay for years and years and years. He was that good a builder.

I remember his boat landing that day when we pulled up to it in the canoe. It had an embankment made of logs. Pete had planted ferns in between the logs, and they hung down, dripping cool blessings on us.

The dock he made lasted for decades, and in fact it was still standing when I later returned to the island.

We went for the funeral feast of a woman who had once saved my father's life, and he felt obligated to go. It was a long, dangerous trip in an open canoe.

When we got to North Fox, I remember my mother jumping out of the canoe and dancing up and down the shoreline. At the time, I thought it was because she was so glad to be on land, but now I think that she probably had kinks in her legs.

When it came time to leave, my mother had the canoe packed, and she said, "Run and get your father," and so I did. My father was standing on the point of North Fox looking out toward Amik, and I saw fear on his face, and up until then I had thought he was invincible. I remember thinking, "My father could be afraid of something?" I had never imagined this could be. I used to ride on his shoulders and felt that I kind of helped rule the world with him.

One of my mother's objections to the journey had been her desire to keep me from contact with the "pagan" religion, for she was the daughter of an Anglican missionary. Accordingly, I was left in the care of Peter Manidu's son, Joe Pete, who was not much older than my own seven years. He, too, had been told that he could not attend the feast, and neither of us liked the situation, but disobedience was not part of our upbringing.

However, Joe Pete threatened to lock me into a small cellar under a trapdoor in the middle of the cabin floor if I didn't behave. Frightened, I ran off down the woodland cart trail in the direction my parents had disappeared. Joe Pete chased after me, but I eluded him by lying flat on my stomach in a large patch of bracken. He went back and forth several times and then returned to the cabin, leaving me to continue down the cart trail.

This trail led through deep woods to the lumber camp triangle and from there to the Harbor of Refuge, where the village of Miniss Kitigan was located.

On the trail, which seemed very long, I met people only once, a family group traveling in the opposite direction. I could see they had been to the feast, for they were carrying food away. The mother of the group came up to me, making "mother" noises. She asked if I were lost, I answered that I was not lost and was going to join my parents at the funeral feast. She asked who my parents were, and I told her. There was an old woman at the end of the group, very unkempt and dirty. Coming abreast of me, she stopped and spoke to me; she had no teeth and foul breath.

"I knew your grandmother, Ikweysens [little girl]," she said. "I knew also *her* grandmother, your father's mother, and your father's mother's mother. They were good women, all of them, and I can see that you are truly their descendant. All of them had a great gift of healing. You must keep your heart happy so that you can also call forth the good spirits for healing." She might have told me much of my forebears, but at the time I wished only that the woman would pass along, even though my home training enabled me to face her courteously and directly. That chance meeting marked a turning point in my life [and a new path for my future].

Long before I reached my destination, I could hear the sound of a great drum and the rise and fall of many voices. It echoed from the bay behind Little Island and sounded like two drums and thousands of people, a sound unknown, which reached out to create a spirit throbbing in my blood. Rounding Catfish Cove and climbing the rise above the village, I saw a cortege of men bared to the waist carrying the body of my father's savior toward the northwest (the direction in which both the traditional and the Christian cemeteries lay) and a multitude of people retiring the Drum to the East.

"Baum! Home!" the muffled, slow-measured Drum said. "Little-Walks-With-Bears-Woman, welcome to your heart's home. Bawm! Bawm! Home! Home!" This was my first sight of a large group of people moving rhythmically to a drum. I had never danced. My maternal grandfather felt dancing was sinful. But without hesitation I began dancing with a group of girls my own age who were in the procession retiring the Drum to the East. It was there that a greatly disturbed Mother found me, scolded me thoroughly, and laid on me the punishment of learning a chapter of scripture—the 121st Psalm. It was duly learned . . . to the rhythm of the Drum, which still beat inside my brain.

"I will lift mine eyes up to the hills" . . . "boom da boom da boom da boom." Nothing else mattered. It had Happened; The Drum has guided my life ever since.

(Journal of Beaver Island History 2 [1980]: 33–35.
Reprinted in part with permission from the Beaver Island Historical Society)

THE STORY OF NANABOOZHOO AND THE BAG OF WINDS

This story happens back in Time's beginning. It is not a sacred story, but we thank the people who keep it alive, especially for us.

It was in the time when our great folk hero, the alternately happy and unhappy Nanaboozhoo, lived upon this Earth. He, who was part spirit and part human. It was bad enough to be part human. But to be part spirit and part human was a very difficult thing. I'd like to repeat that just in case anybody should not have stumbled upon that fact, that *that* is what Nanaboozhoo represents. I didn't. Somehow or other, nobody pointed that out to me when I was young. I am sorry they didn't. I am sorry I wasn't smart enough to catch onto that. Because of his dual nature, Nanaboozhoo was always in trouble here and there. Because of his dual nature, he always had compassion. Because of his dual nature, he was always trying big foolish things and silly little things. And I didn't realize that he represented ourselves, humankind. Because we, too, are part human and part divine.

Now in those days when Nanaboozhoo walked this Earth and this area the people lived along the shoreline . . . probably the precursors of the people we call the Ojibway now . . . and gathered most of their living from the lake. They made excellent canoes, and they made wonderful nets. They also were very careful about honoring the fish people and keeping the promise that our ancestors made to bury their bones respectfully. But they had an awful time getting those fish because way back at that time, although the Sun was set in his order, the winds had never been set in their order. And the winds just blew this way and that way and up and down and back and forth and cross-ways and east, west, north, and south. Or stopped and went round and round in a circle. They never knew what was going to happen, so a good and earnest father who set out upon the lake to garner food for his family risked his life whenever he went out because he never knew when the wind was going to blow up and whether he was ever going to come home again. The people who lived along the lakes, they thought that wasn't right. They said it ought to be like other things . . . that if you say your prayers and you work hard and you are sincere of heart and effort you should be able to sort of gauge how things were going to happen out.

But they didn't know what they could do about the winds because, of course, they were just human beings. And though they said their prayers, it didn't seem to make an awful lot of difference.

Well, one night when they were palavering about the campfire on this, somebody said, "Well, why don't we talk with Nanaboozhoo? Because you know, Nanaboozhoo is the Son of the West Wind, and that makes him part spirit. He's got a real 'in' with the West Wind. Maybe he can do something to help us."

And the people all said, "Hey, that's a wonderful idea. What can we do? What kind of gifts can we make to show him how earnest we are?"

Now, you know, Nanaboozhoo was a giant of a creature. Big. He could put one foot on one of those little islands and step straight across the Straits of Mackinac. He used to like to come to the area because of the sand dunes. It was a really comfortable place for him to rest his big, long body . . . put his feet up on one end, lay his head down at the other. People would often find places where he had done that. They knew he'd been there because they could see where his giant buttocks were and they could see where he rested his head and where he kicked his feet, and then they would look at each other and say, "Ah, Nanaboozhoo was here."

So they said, "Well, we'll make him the kind of things we like because the human side of him will like those gifts." And so the women set to work, and they made a giant pair of leggings that would stretch over Nanaboozhoo's very very long legs . . . because he was always striding through the forests, which came up to his thighs, like bushes come up to ours.

And the men said, "What will . . . ? We'll catch a buffalo and make a big pie for him because he likes to eat a lot and he has trouble getting enough food for that giant body of his." And those were both very good choices.

It took them a very long time to work on that because there were very few buffalo that wandered into this area. And it took a long time to cure and cut those long leggings. They had to find a place where Nanaboozhoo had rested in the sand dunes so they could measure the size big enough to fit him. Then one day when the winds began to blow and they heard huge shouts on the wind that were almost like a spirit calling, they said, "Nanaboozhoo comes."

And so Nanaboozhoo came, whistling and jumping over the Straits of Mackinac with his little waboose [bunny rabbit] riding in his hind pocket, and laid himself out in the sand dunes. And the people said, "He's here now, he's here now. We'll go talk with him." So they got together, and one very strong person carried the drum. They had to take six ladies to carry one legging and six ladies to carry the other legging and twelve men to carry that little pie . . . that "little" buffalo pie. They left the forest and climbed the sand dune, and when they got to the top they lit their torches and they marched to where Nanaboozhoo was sleeping in the sand dunes, chanting so that he'd wake up and hear what they had to say.

And Nanaboozhoo, who was sleepy, heard this chanting and he saw these pricks of light coming, and he kind of woke himself up and said, "Whoa, whoa." Sand just blew around all everywhere with his breath. "Who comes? What do you want?"

The spokesman for the people who lived along the shoreline stepped out timidly and said, "Ho, Nanaboozhoo, son of the West Wind and an Anishinaabe woman. We come to ask a favor of you. We, your human Anishinaabe brothers."

"Oh," said Nanaboozhoo. "Why should I do a favor for you?"

"Well," said the speaker, who was trained to be a diplomat, "because we are indeed your blood brothers and part of you and because we are a people in much need. And you are the only being we know that has so strong a contact with the spirits." And the ladies scuttled forward and laid down one legging and ladies scuttled forward and laid down another legging, and sure enough they were just right for the long size of Nanaboozhoo. And the men grunted and groaned, and they lugged forward this giant buffalo pie and put it down. When Nanaboozhoo saw these gifts he knew that these people had worked a long time to make these big enough for him, and he was much touched by their gifts.

"Well," he said. He sat up and the sand and the wind and his breath splattered around all over everybody, and everyone fell back but nobody went away. "What can I do for you, my little human brethren?"

"Well," said the speaker, "We have this great problem . . . the winds in this place. They blow this way and they blow that way and they blow up and down, and they roll around and around and around and they blow backward and forward and we never know where they are going to blow. There is no system to it at all. You can't figure it out. Now you know we depend for our livelihood a great deal upon the fish that our nets bring in. But we never know when we set out whether we will come home again. And we thought you could bring it to the attention of the spirits that there ought to be some sort of system and an order whereby a good, sincere, honest worker could tell if it was a good time to go out or bad time to go out. Was he going to haul in the fish or was it likely to mean his own life and leave his family defenseless? And we thought if Creation hasn't somehow—the Seven Grandfathers hadn't somehow—thought to order that, maybe they could order it like the waters and the sun and the moon are ordered."

Nanaboozhoo said, "Ungh." Then he got a whiff of that pie, and he said, "Mmmm. Well, a gift like this certainly deserves some consideration, and I promise you, after I have had a little time to enjoy this gift of yours, I will put on these leggings and I will go and talk to my father the West Wind to see what can be done."

Oh, the people they uvulated [cheered] and they clapped and they shouted and they danced and they thanked him a thousand times. They went home that night really reassured because Nanaboozhoo had seemed so compassionate. I'm going to tell you that Nanaboozhoo kept his word to his human brothers. He put on his leggings and he strode in them and they were wonderful protection. The trees didn't scratch his legs so much. And he ate that pie so fast that people watching from afar couldn't believe it.

Then he disappeared, and everybody said, "Now he's gone to talk to the West Wind." That, indeed, is what he had done.

He stood on the highest dune and looked out and called upon his father the West Wind and said, "Oh, my father. These little people, these little brethren of mine, they have asked me for a favor . . . to speak to you on their behalf. And they pointed out something I never thought about before, and I don't know whether the Seven Grandfathers have thought about it before either. But you know . . . every time they set out in the boats they risk their lives. It's the way they get most of their livelihood. This is the way they subsist, they get their sustenance from the fish of the lakes. For which they are truly grateful, and they do keep the commandment that the bones should be buried with honor like a fallen warrior. They still lose their menfolk time after time because they can't tell whether the waves are going to be big or little or whether there is going to be a big blow of wind or whether there is going to be a soft wind, a little wind, a big wind, or a hurricane. Now, they don't ask to be excused from difficulties and dangers. They only ask that there be some order to the winds like there is to the sun and the moon and the waters. So I told them I would speak to you about this and you would carry this message to the Seven Grandfathers, I hoped. Will you do that for us and for my little human brethren?"

Nanaboozhoo's father, the West Wind, we know from other Nanaboozhoo stories, was quite accustomed to getting very strange requests from his son, Nanaboozhoo. This time he was really moved by the request because he wasn't asking anything at all for Nanaboozhoo. He was only asking something for his little human brethren, and the West Wind remembered the beauty of Nanaboozhoo's mother, and he said, "Oh, that is indeed a reasonable request. My son, I am proud of your asking. I will carry the message to the Seven Grandfathers. Come back to this same place tomorrow night and I will speak with you about it."

Then the West Wind was gone. Nanaboozhoo was feeling really good about that. He was in one of his high ego moods and he went around saying, "I am Nanaboozhoo, son of the West Wind and an Anishinaabe woman. Ho, ho, I am Nanaboozhoo. I am going to do something to help my little brethren." And the next night, after he had consumed the last of that gigantic buffalo pie, and a whole buffalo had gone into it, mind you, he went back and stood on that same dune, and sure enough his father the West Wind came roaring out of the west. He greeted Nanaboozhoo before Nanaboozhoo even had time to greet him, which was unusual.

The West Wind was very happy that he had asked that kind of thing. And he told Nanaboozhoo, "The Seven Grandfathers also thought that there should be some sort of order to the winds that blow along the shoreline. There shouldn't be Noodi-nun [winds] that blow here and blow there, around and around in circles like little damselfish."

Nanaboozhoo said, "That's good. That's fine. So you'll do something about it."

"No," said his father the West Wind, "you'll do something about it. You're the one that was petitioned. You fix it." And the West Wind was gone.

So, from being highly elated, poor, gigantic, powerful Nanaboozhoo was thoroughly deflated. He sat there in that sand dune all by himself and said, "I, do something about it? I am not the one that's the mighty spirit. You're the one that's the mighty spirit. What can I do?"

Then he listened, and far away he heard his father's voice rumbling in the distant clouds, "Do something about it. Do something about it."

Nanaboozhoo sat there and he thought and thought and he went to sleep thinking about it. When the sun rose the next morning, he had an idea. So, when he heard his little brethren coming up from the villages along the shoreline, [he said to himself] "I've got to tell them something. I've got to tell them something. These people gave me gifts [from the] buffalo and they really are sincere and they really are depending on me." He looked down at his leggings, and the whole form of his leg just popped up clear in his head. And he said to the shoreline dweller, the Agaminuck, "This is going to be a hard job, but it's important for you to do. I want all of you—the men are to help with this, don't lay it all on the women. It will take the labor of the men and the women together. You are to make the top of a gigantic bag. Now, it is important that you do a real good job because it's the part that is going to be your help. Also I am going to go to the Heartlands to ask the Odawa to make part of it. You want your part to be better than theirs, right?"

And the Ojibway said, "Oh, yes. We want our part to be better."

"Now, it's got to be very big and very long, as far as the

82

sand dunes stretch, from the Straits of Mackinac all the way down to Ogema (Houghton Lake)."

"Oh, we can never get that many together."

He said, "If you want this to work, you will."

So they set to work, and they stretched and they dried and they sewed and they pierced and they put in a drawstring that was the most gigantic rope you ever saw. And Nanaboozhoo stood up there and he saw all their busyness and the work they were doing and how they were putting this together, and they really were going to do it.

He said, "Oh, ho, ho. This is good. I will go now and talk to the Odawa." So he took several big steps across those sand dunes, and where his gigantic footprint stepped there are the lakes: Lake Burt, Lake Torch, and a lake called Lake Otsego. He pressed in that hard. He came at last to where the Odawa lived, and he said, "Ho, Mighty Nation, the Odawa, Nanaboozhoo salutes you."

And the Odawa stopped; they had never asked for anything particularly, and they couldn't believe that Nanaboozhoo was talking to them.

Some of them said, "We just think we heard that. That's the way the thunder sounds sometimes."

Then he asked them again. "Ho, Odawa, Nanaboozhoo salutes you, Kid Animikan" [I salute you], and they *had* to stop their business and look up.

Their Speaker trembled but had to stand forward and say, "Oh, Mighty Nanaboozhoo, the Odawa salute you. Why are we honored by your great presence?"

Nanaboozhoo said, "I have need for your services."

They said, "You have need for OUR services? How could that be?"

Nanaboozhoo said, "The people of the Ojibway have come to me and made petition and asked that it be arranged with the spirits that there be some order to the winds. They shouldn't go crazy, willy-nilly and around and around, but a person should have some idea of where the wind is going to blow from on any given day. So I am going to do something that will be as much help to you as it is for your brothers that live along the shoreline. What I need for you to do is this. The Ojibway are making a gigantic top for a gigantic bag. . . . one that stretches all the way from Mackinac to Houghton Lake. The drawstring is a gigantic rope. Nobody but Nanaboozhoo could draw it shut. Now, all very well for somebody to be skilled [enough] to make a rope like that, but you know there has to be a really sturdy, strong belly to this bag if it is going to hold anything at all."

And they said, "Oh, yes, a bag that big. It would have to be."

Nanaboozhoo said, "I want you all to get very busy because there are more buffalo on the plains in the middle of the state. I want you to make the center part of this bag. And it has to be very, very strong because that part is really going to take the strain. And you would want your part to be the very best. You would want it to be better than the drawstring part that the Ojibway are making."

The Odawa said, "Oh, yes. That's right and we are very good at this sort of thing. . . . the strong center part of the bag that will take the strain. Yes, Nanaboozhoo, we'll get busy on that right away."

"Very good," said Nanaboozhoo. "I am going over to the far side of this great land, along Lake Huron, and I am going to talk to your brothers the Potawatomi. While I am gone you get busy and get that done and let everything else go and get it done as fast as you can."

The Odawa said, "Yes, we'll do that for you, Nanaboozhoo." And they surely did. They took the strong hides that they had been planning on using to make wigwams for the winter and they went out hunting for some extra. They put a really big effort out because they knew they were providing the part of the bag where the biggest strain would come.

Nanaboozhoo went stepping on across the land. He walked along the river that is called the Grand River and the Washtenaw [Huron River] and made great valleys where his giant footsteps went. And he got to the other side, and he called out and said, "Ho, Bodowadameg, you Dwellers of the Forest. I am Nanaboozhoo. I greet you. I greet you with the voice of Animkeeg [the Thunderers]. Kid Animikan!"

The Potawatomi [Bodowadameg] heard this, and said, "My goodness, if that thunder doesn't sound like somebody talking." But of course it wasn't. It just happened to sound like that, and they went on about their business.

So again he called, saying, "Ho, Nation of the People of the Fire. Nanaboozhoo greets you."

Finally they had to acknowledge it. Their frightened and trembling Speaker stood forward and said, "We think we hear you speaking, Nanaboozhoo. But, Nanaboozhoo, you are part spirit. Why would the likes of you call upon the Potawatomi?"

Nanaboozhoo said, "I have already called upon your brothers, the Ojibway and the Odawa." And he told them the story, and he said, "Now, what I need of you . . . I need you to make the bottom of a bag . . . a bag that will be sturdy and strong and stretch from the Straits of Mackinac to Houghton Lake."

The Potawatomi said, "We can't do anything like that."

Nanaboozhoo said, "Well, the Ojibway can."

And the Potawatomi said, "Oh, they can? They can make something that big?"

"Oh, yes," said Nanaboozhoo. "They are making the drawstring and the top of this gigantic bag. It is going to be very good, indeed. Fine rope, fine rope those Ojibway make. And the Odawa. They are going to make the belly of the bag. They are hunting buffalo on the plains of their land right now."

"Hmmm," said the Potawatomi. "If the Ojibway and the Odawa are going to do it, I guess maybe we'd better do something too. What's that you say? You want us to make the bottom? Closed up? We don't have to make rope or anything?"

"No," said Nanaboozhoo, "you got out of this real easy. All you have to do is make the bottom part of this bag. I already told you how big it's got to be. I want you to stop everything you are doing and work on it—man, woman and child. Because I am

Nanaboozhoo, son of the West Wind and an Anishinaabe woman, and this is my desire."

The Potawatomi said, "Well, if it's what you want us to do, we'll do the very best we can, Nanaboozhoo."

"Then," said Nanaboozhoo, "I will be back after the sun rises and sets seven times."

Then he went whistling back down the Grand River Valley, chuckling to himself and knocking over trees with his big legs and leggings as he went. For he thought he had a fine idea here. And when the sun had risen and set seven times he went to the Ojibway and said, "Do you have the top of the bag ready?" The Ojibway had worked and worked and worked and had made a big, strong, cedar rope. It was so big most of them had never seen anything as big as that. That was the drawstring for the bag. They cured the hides and they made the holes and they laced this gigantic rope through it, and of course none of them could draw it shut.

But Nanaboozhoo just leaned over and picked up one end and pushed and pulled, and I tell you the top of that bag was so big and the rope was so thick and so strong that it took fourteen tries for Nanaboozhoo to pull it shut. So you know how big it was!

"Very good, Ojibway," Nanaboozhoo said. "Now I leave. You must let me take this and carry it to the Heartland People."

The Ojibway said, "Hey, anything that's going to help us we'll appreciate. We're glad you like this."

Nanaboozhoo picked up this great top, part-drawstring part-gigantic bag, and he pulled it back over the place where he had walked, and that made the grooves in the valley that now contains the Washtenaw [Huron] even bigger.

Then he came to the Heartland People. They had been working and hunting and curing and stitching together the center part. They even had to make extra special needles and extra special piercing equipment so they could sew these together. It took two men with gigantic stone hammers to drive the holes so they could stitch it, you know. It was that big. When he brought them the top and plopped it down, they looked at it, and the people had to run this way and that way so it wouldn't fall on them.

"Now, I want you to sew the top to this very strong belly you have made for the bag."

And the Odawa said, "That's awful big for us. To get to the top of that bag, it would be like climbing a hill. How are we going to get the overlapping stitches in there?"

Nanaboozhoo said, "You go get the hardest hickory tree you can find."

So they said, "Well, we know where that is. What are you going to do with it?"

Nanaboozhoo said, "Show it to me." And they did. Nanaboozhoo took that hickory tree, and he pulled it right straight out of the earth and took off the branches like they were little twigs. The people just stood there aghast because they knew how strong and tough that wood was. He made it into the greatest skin piercer you ever saw . . . big and strong and shiny. Then he said, "Now, you lay the skins together. Have all your strong men hold it there, and have your strong women bring the strongest sinew they have and I'll pound the holes."

So, in that manner, with Nanaboozhoo pounding the holes, the Odawa men and women pushed the lacings through on this thick, heavy belly of the bag that they had made. And when they got through with that it was the biggest, strongest bag that any of them could possibly imagine. It was so big that it made a great big saucer in the earth where it rested. And that is where the body of Houghton Lake is now.

Nanaboozhoo took the top part of the belly of the bag, fastened together, and he dragged it along the valley of the Grand River until he got to the far side of the land, and there were the Potawatomi, working very hard.

They apologized and said, "Nanaboozhoo, we don't know. But we've done the very best we can. We're not sure at all. YOU know this is not the kind of thing we're accustomed to doing. We do most of our building with birchbark and elm and we . . .

well. . . . Here, look at what we have done and see what you think."

They had made the bottom of that bag so big that it ended in the valley of the great AuSable.[1] And Nanaboozhoo looked at that, and he was very pleased because he knew that the natural tendency of the Potawatomi was to make more fancy, decorative things and not such big, strong things. They liked to do woodwork instead of working with skins. He was very pleased with the way they had worked hard.

He said, "Now I want you to help me lace this on." He gave them the same kind of orders that he had given the Odawa, and they did the same thing as the Odawa.

They said, "You know we can't possibly do that. We don't have needles that big, and we don't have sinews that long."

Nanaboozhoo, contrary to his usual manner, was very kind and patient. He told them, "We're going to lace it together." So the Potawatomi and Nanaboozhoo together laced that bottom on that gigantic bag, and when it was finished all the people marveled.

And Nanaboozhoo said, "Now I will take this back to the far shore of Lake Michigan. You'll know whether my idea works or not and whether the petition of the Ojibway has been heard because you, too, will benefit from the order of the winds."

The Potawatomi said, "Oh, thank you, Nanaboozhoo. Thank you."

So he took that gigantic bag and he dragged it back across the state, and he dragged that bag behind him where he had walked over first, then back again. It opened up the great valley of the Grand River . . . the longest river in our state.[2] The water from one side rushed in right behind his heels. He didn't pay much attention to that because he was too busy thinking about

1. The AuSable River flows eastward into Lake Huron. It reaches the lake at the town of Oscoda.
2. The Grand River begins in the city of Jackson, flowing north to Grand Rapids, where it turns westward to flow into Lake Michigan.

what he was going to do next, but the people noticed it. They had to get out of the way as the water rushed by. Then they saw that it was going to make a great waterway that stretched from one side of the state to the other. Then, true to the Potawatomi's way of doing things, before the water had even settled in they started thinking about how many canoes they could make and how far the canoes could travel and how long the river was and how many days it would take them to use it.

Now, when Nanaboozhoo got back to the Lake Michigan side and threw down the gigantic bag that the Three Fires Tribes had made together, he said, "There, there you are."

The people looked at it and they marveled and they thanked him, although they had no idea what they were supposed to be thanking him for. They said, "That's very great. That's wonderful, that's very marvelous, Nanaboozhoo, but what do we do with it?"

Nanaboozhoo said, "Uh, uh. What do you do with it? Well, uh, what you do with it is you, do, uh . . . get some trees and prop the mouth of it open and you get some rocks and put them in the base end and then we invite the winds to go in." So partly out of pride and partly out of fear, the Ojibway got busy and did just that.

Then they said, "OK, now we're going to go home and cover our heads, Nanaboozhoo. You fix it."

One of the things that was troublesome for him—and for the beings that lived on this Earth—was that Nanaboozhoo didn't always think things through very carefully. The human side of him just never seemed to be able to carry through what the spirit side of him cooked up. So he stood there, and he looked in the great cave of a bag, and he said, "All right, winds, come on in." And the winds went whistling by and down the shoreline, making big waves and making little whirlwinds and blew off the tops of the trees around him and said, "Ha, ha, ha, ha." And no matter what Nanaboozhoo said or did, or which songs he sang or what, he couldn't get the winds to go in that giant bag.

He was very discouraged, as Nanaboozhoo often became.

He was completely disconsolate. He said, "What have I done now? I have got all of these people who are depending on me thinking I am a big shot and that I can take care of this for them. And the winds, those same winds, those same silly naughty winds, they are not paying any attention. They don't know who I am, and they are not paying any attention."

While he was complaining and carrying on like a gigantic spoiled child he saw little Meligisik, the little gust whirlwinds . . . the little teeny tiny ones that you see go puffing around in the autumn, just lift a few leaves or a little bit of dust . . . whirling around "la dee dee dah, la dee dee dee dah."

Nanaboozhoo looked at him and said, "If only I had a big one of those that I could get into my bag. Come, Meligisik-wenhs, will you dance into my bag? See, I have made for you a gigantic dance hall, the biggest wigwam you can imagine. Just for you, little Meligisik. You come and you invite your friends and you dance inside it first, will you, please? Will you dance up and down and make the bag jump up and down? If you do that, all the winds that are around, they will see that you are a brave one to dive in there. And they'll want to come in and see what you are doing."

So that little dust whirlwind (you must say thanks every time you see one of them reeling along, doing their little miniature blowing) danced right into the mouth of the bag. Then the big bag began to jump up and down.

Nanaboozhoo said to the other winds, who were just whistling here or there all around, "Hey, You Winds, big meeting of Wind Peoples going on here in this gigantic bag. They are having a great powwow. If you listen, you can hear them whistling. You can see the bag jumping up and down. Now, you guys, you don't want to miss any of that. You don't want to leave it up to the little wehbidehbig, just let them do all the deciding what the winds are going to be like and what they're going to do. You'd better get in there and kind of take charge of things, don't you think?"

So the Winds from the East and the Winds from the South

and the Winds from the West and the Winds from the North said, "That's right. WE can't let those little dust whirlwinds take charge of all the wind discussions around here. We'll go in and show them how a powwow ought to be done and how a council ought to be held." And they whistled into the bag.

"Aha," said Nanaboozhoo, "now for the strong winds that blow out of Keewaydin [the northwest]." He used the same technique to get the winds of Keewaydin, those that bring the cold in the winter and the great winter blasts, to go in and confer with the rest of the winds. The bag got bigger and bigger and bigger, and it began to stretch and it began to dance up and down and to heave and to jump back and forth. When all the winds were inside of that bag and Nanaboozhoo had taken hold of that gigantic drawstring, which was really a great thick rope, he pulled on it with all the strength that he had and he closed it in tight. And the winds of Lake Michigan, all of them, were contained therein.

Oh, the rejoicing call of Nanaboozhoo sounded across the dunes and down the lakeshore, and the people knew that something great and good had happened and they all gave thanks, but they didn't know for what. Nanaboozhoo stood there, and he stood there, and the bag heaved and pushed and shoved and moved back and forth and danced up and down. Sometimes it looked as if it might break, but it didn't. But you could see the strain on it . . . pushing, jumping, pulling, turning around and around.

Nanaboozhoo said, "I've done a great job. I've got them all captured in here and uh . . . I'll. . . . Dear Father, what shall I do with them?"

And the voice of his father said, "Can't expect me to tell you. You caught me in that bag, too."

"Oh," said Nanaboozhoo, "shall I let you out?"

"No," said the West Wind. "My place is with the other winds. Your place is to decide what to do."

Nanaboozhoo looked up in despair and looked all around and he saw the great, long, blue expanse of the lake, which was now very calm, and no little chinooks were dancing wildly up and down the shoreline and the Ojibway were feverishly getting out their canoes and saying, "Oh, look, look, look! There is no wind. We've got to get fish while we can."

Nanaboozhoo said, "Well, that's the place for it to go, 'cause if I leave it here . . . let that blast out of the bag here . . . it's going to knock down all the forest and then the people will have no way to subsist." So he took the great rope and pulled that bag of winds into Lake Michigan, where it floated. Nanaboozhoo climbed onto the top of it and like a silly little boy began to kick his feet and paddle with his hands. Since there were no winds to disturb [the lake], he went floating along and playing and having the best time in the water. After he got a ways out on Lake Michigan, he realized that, my goodness, he was way out there and he still didn't know what to do with the bag. He looked up and he saw an island, and the island that he saw was Miniss Susheegan, the one out here that is called Fog Island now.

"Ha, that's what I'll do. I'll take this big bag and I'll set it down out on the Island of Bass Fish and leave it there and it won't bother anybody." So he started paddling in that direction. The bass and whitefish were the highest fish people upon whom the two-leggeds depended the most. They were very afraid and very smart fish, especially the Bass People. And their guardians and their scouts picked up on this great current that was out there in the lake and coming in their direction.

They said to their elders, "Somebody's got to do something because this great danger is headed right for our homeland!" So a whole school of Bass Elders swam out to meet Nanaboozhoo and the gigantic creation he was floating on. And they said, "Ho, Nanaboozhoo, son of the West Wind and an Anishinaabe woman. You are out for a play on this lovely calm day?"

Nanaboozhoo said, "Play? I have captured all the winds that come along the shoreline. They are in this bag. I am going to take them out to Miniss Susheegan and leave them there."

They said, "That's what we were afraid of. We caught the

waving and underwater sounds, and you know this is the season of the year when we are filling up our nesting places with eggs. The water there is getting muddy and the silt is covering up some of our young and our fingerlings won't be able to come out. We have come to ask you if you won't take your play toy or whatever it is you're splashing around with, take it someplace else, and don't disturb us, because you know not only do we have to have clean clear water for the continuance of our own kind but the two-leggeds, they depend on us for subsistence and we can't have our babies killed."

Nanaboozhoo said, "Oh, well, yeah, yeah, right. Thank you for bringing that up. I really hadn't thought about that. You're very famous. Yes, the two-leggeds do indeed depend on you. I wouldn't want to do anything that would harm your nation. But what am I going to do with that gigantic bag?"

The Fish Elders said, "Oh, we don't know about that. That's your job, oh, Mighty Son of West Wind. But don't, we beg you, bring it to our island." Nanaboozhoo looked up and saw another island. It was Amikogenda, the Place of the Beaver.

"That's all right. I can't destroy the food place for the people because after all the whole idea of doing this is to make it so they can catch fish. And I'd be stupid to make it so they can't do that. I'll just take it over to Amikogenda, and drop the bag off over there." So he started paddling in that direction.

It was the springtime, and they [Amikwag, the beavers] had just made new dams and some new ponds, and they had made a whole bunch of new houses, and they heard the rush of Nanaboozhoo's paddling and the roar of the winds inside the giant bag. They said, "What's going to happen? That's going to destroy everything that we've built . . . our colonies and our dams and our sluiceways [water that flows around a dam]."

They gathered warriors together and they sent a whole group of them out to meet Nanaboozhoo, and they said, "Oh, Mighty Son of West Wind, Nanaboozhoo, we salute you," and they all slapped their tails. Oh, what a sound that was. Then they told him, "We saw you coming our way and we just built all these new dams and all these new sluiceways and these new ponds and we put up a whole bunch of these new lodges. We have young inside of them, and we have come to ask you . . . please, Nanaboozhoo, don't put that thing—whatever it is that you are playing with—don't leave it on our land. It will cover it all up, and our babies will be slaughtered."

Nanaboozhoo said, "Oh, no. Not again. Well, I can see your point, Amikwag. But what am I going to do with this thing?"

They looked at him, and they said, "We don't know, but we beg you, we petition you, don't bring it to our homeland."

Nanaboozhoo was kind of tired of this game by this time, and he thought, "I am going to put this thing the first place I can." He looked up and saw another island. It was getting toward twilight, and he said, "I'm going to be clever and sly this time. I am going to sneak up on Kitiganing Island and I'm not going to let anything . . . whatever beings are there . . . I'm not going to let them know I'm coming."

And he didn't paddle, and he didn't kick. He just glided along quietly on the top of the water. Before anything that lived on Kitiganing Island had a chance to even realize what was going on, Nanaboozhoo had put his foot on Kitiganing Island . . . the place where the two lakes are now.

So before anyone could say, "Please don't do that, Nanaboozhoo," he was gone. Oh, he was gone so far and so fast that nothing could call out to him.

And there the giant bag lay. And it lay and it lay. The Ojibway people were very happy and the Odawa were very happy and the Potawatomi were very happy. The bass fish of Miniss Susheegan, oh, they were very happy. They hatched out their fingerlings . . . hundreds of them. They made the water at the bottom of the lake dark with their bodies. The Amikwag were very happy, too.

The beings of Kitiganing Island poked at the giant bag and said, "What's this? What is lying on top of our land?" Poke, poke. They called, "Does anybody know what this is?" And nobody answered.

But they heard voices inside that said, "Let us out, let us out."

After a long, long time, when the waters of Lake Michigan were very smooth and peaceful, one little place began to spring open on the side of the bag. Then another little place. Then one of the little Meligisik slipped right out through that small hole and made it bigger. Out came the winds with a great rush!

That is why you can never tell which way the wind is going to blow on Kitiganing Island. Sometimes it blows north to south, east to west. But it also blows west to south and south to east and east to north. And sometimes it goes round and around and around. We get all kinds of wabishwug. So if you want to be on Kitiganing Island you'll have to talk to the Spirits for your safety because the winds won't give it to you.

Ancestors

My Maternal Grandfather Comes to America, the Needlepoint Tapestry

When my Grandfather Moorhouse was a little boy, his mother came back from a shopping trip. Francis wondered what she had brought him and seemed so disappointed when she did not immediately hand over a gift that later she took a needlepoint pattern that she had picked up on her trip and, after tearing it into little irregularly shaped pieces, presented it to him as a jigsaw puzzle.

Francis put it all together, and he fell in love with the design. It was a full-colored picture, about two feet by three feet, of a woman and two young children standing and listening to a seated man playing a mandolin. He wanted his mother to order the entire needlepoint project, graph and yarn and all. She said to him "Francis, you'll never be able to do this yourself!" But you know what his mother did? She did buy everything needed to do the tapestry and spent some years finishing it.

Finally, on his twenty-first birthday, she presented the finished tapestry to Francis, who was so happy with it. A friend whittled a hand-carved wooden frame for it as a going-away present, using only a penknife. The frame has eight tiers and is composed of hundreds of small pieces of wood. Together with the tapestry, the entire piece measures almost three by four feet and is very heavy. The wood is hard and would have taken many blisters and many blade sharpenings to shape. When Francis came to America, his

The Moorhouse
needlepoint tapestry

beloved framed needlepoint picture came with him. My mother inherited it upon her father's death, and so I grew up with this picture, too. It traveled with us where ever we moved, from a little tiny cabin to a spacious house. It was always packed in a feather tick to keep it safe and is much treasured, especially because of the love that is woven and carved into it.

The colors have only faded slightly, remaining bright and clear. The four people in it are dressed in loose clothes, probably rustic Greek or Italian style, while behind them is a small, flat-roofed structure held up in the front by two white columns. Green vines riot over the building, and green trees and plants fill much of the space. Blue and purple mountains are hinted at in the background. The sky is brighter than any that England ever sees. The frame is truly a wonder to behold.

(As told to Lee Boisvert circa 1987)

When he came to America from Yorkshire, he brought his shovel, which was a gift for his twelfth birthday. The family thought he'd help his mother in the garden. When he got it, they asked, "What will you do with your shovel?" and he replied, "Take it to America."

Francis Hague Moorhouse was the youngest of seven sons. He was twenty-one when he came here the first time. The bulk of the family inheritance and property at Wyncobank, England, went to the oldest son, so Francis, my grandfather, had to learn some kind of trade to earn his living. The family felt that they had tried everything with Francis. They gave him the opportunity to learn all kinds of crafts. He seemed to do well at all of them, but they didn't seem to "take." He couldn't support himself [at any of them]; however, he *was* very good at art.

He was great at playing the violin. He'd take that up in the mill with him. He was supposed to put the bags of grain down the chute and the bags would hit the stones with force and the stones would turn and grind and make the flour and people would catch the flour down below. All of a sudden there wouldn't be any flour. It was because Francis, up in the tower, had forgotten to put the grain in—he was busy playing the violin or drawing a picture or something or other.

Religion

Francis got into religion because Pansy, who worked in the kitchen, said he had this vocational call to be a minister. His folks said no,

The shovel that Grandfather Moorhouse brought from England

they had sponsored him for so many things and nothing ever came of it. If he wanted to be a minister, he could do it on his own; they weren't going to help him. Of course, they never thought he would. But Pansy apparently had slipped him goodies ever since he could remember.

He was sitting at the kitchen table and weeping over the fact that his parents had forbidden him to be a minister, and Pansy said, "Well, you know, if it's God's will, no matter if they are your parents, and I know you owe them a great deal, but they can't stop it. If it's God's will, you will be a minister."

Whether it's what she said or what it was, sure enough, in a couple of years my grandfather was part of the Yorkshire Riding [Circuit]—which means he rode a horse to all these little mission churches—all services. He did so well that they [the church] agreed to take him into ministerial college. Then he had to choose a ministry. It was his Native American ancestry that made him decide he wanted to work in America with the Indians. [He was descended from an English girl who was a deaf-mute. Her parents sent her to America before the American Revolution to find a husband. She eventually married a Native American and moved—along with him and some of their children—back to England.]

Before he left England, a friend of his mother's named Elizabeth Pickering [Elizabeth Pickering was a distant relative of one of the adult children left behind in America when the above ancestor Susanna moved to England with her Native American husband], who belonged to the same church as he did, said, "Now, when you come to America, if by any chance you should go to a place called Michigan, if you should get to an area called Leelanau—which isn't very likely since there's not much there—there's a woman named Susanna Bpgonikwe who lives there with a girl child, and I'd like you to see how the child is doing."

He said, "Would you like me to write to you about her?"

"No," she said. "If you write your mother, your mother will invite me to tea and she will let me read what you've written." I don't think Elizabeth wanted her husband to know about [the child].

By coincidence, my grandfather was assigned to Michigan, to the town of Romeo,[1] which is in the middle of the state. Then he was hired to do some evangelistic work in Saginaw, which on the map looked like it was near Leelanau. So he did indeed come to Leelanau. And he did indeed find Susanna Bpgonikwe, the sister of the lady in England, and her daughter. When he wrote back to his mother and her friend Elizabeth, he said that he had indeed found Susanna Bpgonikwe and the girl child and that she was doing well. In fact, he had married her [the girl child]!

The Moorhouse family didn't know what to make of it. They hadn't thought of his marrying a native person. But they shouldn't have been too prejudiced because of the respect that they showed Susanna—the deaf-mute—and her husband.

When Francis Moorhouse married my grandmother, it was more involved than he thought because when Elizabeth Pickering told him she'd like him to look in on this girl and see how she was doing if he could she hadn't told him that the girl was her daughter.

My Maternal Grandmother

After my missionary grandfather met and married this woman, whose name was Mistequay (Mist-e-quay), he baptized her and named her Margaret. She became the mother of a little boy, Arthur John, the first male child born to that generation of the Moorhouses. That meant a lot to the people in England. They offered to forget the fact that she was a native person if she would come and bring the little boy for them to see. The English family sent the money for the journey, so they went. When they got there, besides the little boy getting acquainted with his grandparents on the Moorhouse side, his mother, Margaret, also got acquainted with her own mother, Elizabeth, and she came to understand some reasons why her mother married James Pickering and did not want to leave England, even after he died.

1. Romeo is on the Saint Clair River in the Thumb area of Michigan.

One reason was that Elizabeth was very, very tall. She had never found anybody that was as tall as she was—she was six foot four. Her husband, James Pickering, was a teacher, and he was six foot four and a half. She didn't want him to bring her back to America; she refused to come.

Finally her grandmother pushed her, "Because we want to go so badly, why won't you come?"

She said, "Well, there are several reasons. One of them is that James Pickering is very dear, and this had been a good place for me. He was good to me, and the people here were good to me, and my life was so much better than it ever was before. I don't want to leave. And the other one is that I want to be buried in the same grave with him." (They do that a lot in Europe.) She said, "I'm not likely to find a grave big enough."

It's true. We have a photograph of the Moorhouse grave, and it's obviously very long.

My maternal grandparents stayed there in England for some years. The little boy they took to see the grandparents died there—little Arthur John. When Arthur John died, they stayed there for two reasons. One was that my grandmother's own mother, Elizabeth Pickering, wouldn't come back to America, and [she and the family] had come to know and like each other, and she'd come to live with them. The other reason was that my grandfather's family couldn't let them go. They gave them a farm, Wyncobank, a place with a beautiful house on it and a granite quarry along the Kanglow River. I have a number of things that came out of Wyncobank. [It is here that Keewaydinoquay's mother was born and lived until she was five years of age.]

My grandfather Francis was a minister when he came back here [to America]. And he got us into a lot of hot water. I look at him, and I think about all the bad scrapes I got into, about not going back on my ideals, and stuff like that. He got into messes like that sometimes. I think of the things my mom told me . . . like the time he refused to burn the Bible. . . .

There were a lot of hard feelings against the Germans during World War I. Terrible things had been said about Germans. In the little town he [my grandfather] taught in, they had asked him to be present at a big bonfire they were going to have and to pray for the war effort. Well, nothing seemed too wrong with that, and all the other ministers were going to be there, so he went. But when he got there what they were doing was burning all the German books that were in town. Anybody who had anything in German, regardless of what it was, was forced to bring it, by the law of the local town council, to a huge bonfire. They had all the ministers sit around it. They went along and gave out books for everybody to put in the fire. When they came to my grandfather, they gave him a red-bound vellum book—the Holy Scriptures in German.

He said, "I can't burn it. This is the word of God, I can't put this in the flames."

The people who were running it [the bonfire event] said, "But this is a German Bible. You can burn that! Ha! Ha!"

There was a big riot . . . people yelling . . . and Reverend Francis Moorhouse was [supposed] to put the first book in the flames. It got really quiet.

He stood up and said, "This book I hold in my hands is the Holy Bible. It's written in the German language, but it is the Holy Bible just the same, and it has an Old Testament and a New Testament and the Concordance and a pronunciation section and a dictionary, and it's the Word of God, no matter what it's written in. I have dedicated my life to the service of God, and Francis Moorhouse will not put the Holy Bible in the flames."

They didn't buy it. He had a really hard time with the church committee. In fact, my mother said he was under suspicion from that time on. When they'd go to a new place, somebody would say something and gossip would get around and the family could tell that somehow something wasn't right . . . that the new people had heard from somebody.

✻ ✻ ✻ ✻

There was a lot of fear and prejudice on both sides that I didn't understand. I remember reading a book in which they told about

German people getting together during the war [World War I] and having secret meetings to stamp on the American flag.

I remember asking my mother, "Why would they stamp on the American flag?"

My mother said, "I can't imagine. There must have been lots of other things to clean your boots on."

I said, "But there must have been some reason they did this, and why would anybody get in trouble for cleaning their boots on the American flag?"

She said, "Some people thought it was their way of showing their hatred for the United States."

And I said, "Well, they were German. . . ." She tried to explain it to me. But what really got me, upset me, so badly [that] they had to come and get me and try to [help me understand was that] the neighbors had a son who [had] died in the war. In their house, there was a little room at the head of the stair, and among the things they had there were the things he'd worn in the war and souvenirs that he'd sent home. Among them was a German helmet—lovely, very sculptured. On the top, it said, "Fur Gott und Der Kaiser."

I remember looking at Mrs. Stevens and saying, "You mean the Germans believe in God?"

She said, "Well, I suppose so, in their way."

My whole head just reeled because I'd heard just one side of this Christian business, and at that time I was so young that I thought that all Christian people loved their brothers and nobody ever turned anybody away, and I couldn't believe that Christian people from this country went to Germany and killed Christian people in Germany. I had thought that these were awful people who worshiped this pagan god called Kaiser.

I remember asking Mrs. Stevens, "Was it like that for everybody? Did all the German soldiers believe in God?"

And she said, "Probably most of them, you know, like our boys are. Some of them do and some don't, but most of them do, some way or another."

I said, "And yet, they went and killed each other?"

She said, "Yes, they did," and she started crying. I guess she was thinking about her son. As little as I was, I realized I was walking on the wrong kind of ground. But this blew me [away].

$$* \quad * \quad * \quad *$$

I remember when the soldiers came home from the war. They were kind of slow getting home, but Indians were likely to take two or three years coming home. They probably stopped at every Indian family between here and wherever they landed.

There would be parties and "welcome homes," and then they would tell about their exploits. They never said anything about killing off another human being and what the details were like. They just told about the exciting things.

Plus the fact that someplace along the way, somebody taught me to say pieces—they called it "a reading—a little verse." I used to do it for all the PTA [Parent-Teacher Association] meetings, and I had quite a reputation for going to the PTA meetings and reciting "little verses" of one kind or another. Among the other places I was invited fairly frequently to say little verses was in the cemeteries . . . on Memorial Day . . . or when someone was interred. There were still bodies coming back from overseas. There would be people there who would remember who was being buried . . . remembered people from those wards.

When I was little, there were people from the Civil War who were still alive. I can remember them very well. There was one old man whose name was Fred Tuck. Everyone called him Colonel. He had run away to join the army when he was sixteen years old. He wasn't quite old enough [to enlist], so he'd run away to join the army anyway. He was a drummer boy. He used to tell me all these fascinating stories. He never told me stories [about the violence], none of that kind of stuff . . . it was just the excitement of running and getting caught and that sort of thing.

Anyway, I used to say these pieces, and people would cry.

I said to my mother, "Why do they ask me to say these pieces if they're only going to cry?"

She said, "It's what they're thinking about when y⌐
They want you to because it was their children."

I remember one time when I said "In Flanders ⌐
Poppies Grow." It didn't mean a thing to me. I was saying a⌐
"row on row," and here was a man whose body had been brought
from Flanders Fields, and his mother wept and wept. I was so disturbed that I could hardly say my little piece.

Paternal Grandparents

MidéOgema knew everything, everything in the whole world. He
was a medicine man. But then, and even now, men didn't have so
much to do with the herbs. Too much work. They had to have a
woman go do it for 'em. So a lot of our finest medicine men lost
their power when their women died. They couldn't recognize the
herbs well enough to do the work of gathering them. Did he try to
help people run their lives so they would be more effective? Yes.
But he did only big healings. Little things, like kids with coughs, he
would have his wife Minissing Odahnikwe (Min-i-sing O-dah-ni-
kwe) go get some herbs. But when it was somebody big and important and male, he would do the healing.

I knew he had at least two wives, which caused my mother to
disapprove of him. She always made it sound like his first wife died
and then he married his second wife, who was such a good grandmother to me. Her name was Minissing Odahnikwe, "Daughter of
the Island." The truth of the matter is he was married to both of
them at the same time. That seemed all right to them. Minissing
Odahnikwe was my father's mother's best girlfriend.

Ni Mishomis MidéOgema always used to say that a man
should have three wives . . . one born in September to bring a warrior son, one born in July so that things would always be managed
well, and one born in May just for enjoyment. My mother did not
approve of her father-in-law speaking this way, but I always felt
that he made some valid points.

(As told to Lee Boisvert circa 1991)

It was a valuable marriage just the same, and all the people involved thought so. There was no difference between my grandfather's children by his first wife and his second wife. The children called them both Mother and MidéOgema Father. If one of them hadn't died, I wouldn't have thought to ask which was my natural grandmother.

When my father's mother [MidéOgema's first wife] died, Minissing Odahnikwe adopted him so if anything ever happened to her husband she would have the right to finish raising the boy.

Minissing Odahnikwe was the best grandmother anybody ever had. When I went, not too long ago, to write down my bloodline so I could qualify for a scholarship so I could work on my doctorate, when I got to Minissing Odahnikwe my pen stopped. According to their (the university's) way, she wouldn't be my grandmother. But in every other way she was.

She taught me a great portion of the Indian songs I know. She told me stories. She taught me how to dance; she showed me how to cook on an open fire. She was a big, jolly woman. She did most of her cooking on an old oil can. She got kids to help her with all kinds of stuff. She'd invent games and give prizes. She always had a bevy of kids around. Nobody minded, and she didn't mind. I went to visit them often. They never stayed put.

My mother used to complain about that. We'd spend half the vacation trying to find [out] where they were. MidéOgema lived in Grand River, the part that stretches very close to Lake Michigan, in the area near Muskegon County in Michigan. But there came a time when he felt the Grand River Ottawa had sold out to Christianity, lock, stock and barrel, and there was no longer any point in staying in Grand River and praying for people who didn't want to be prayed for and who wanted to pay you for making prayers. He said native peoples no longer respected the old ways and they thought the missionaries knew everything and [they] did everything [the missionaries] said. They didn't know the missionaries were with the white government people, who were rooking them out of everything.

So he moved north, up the coast of Michigan. I think he went to Pentwater, which was up the shoreline, and then they moved to somewhere near Good Hart,[2] and then he moved out to Kitiganing Island. Both of his wives were from Kitiganing Island. He was like the old patriarch, with two wives.

Then there was the time he got mad at the president of the United States. He felt that the president was misusing his power with the Indian agents. Grandfather felt that if the president understood, he would do things differently. So he wrote the president a number of letters about how things really were. He made a big fuss about the first letter he sent. The second he had written for him because he thought maybe the president couldn't read his handwriting. In the third, he threatened to leave the United States if the president didn't do something about it. Well, the president didn't even acknowledge his letter, much less do anything about it. Since everyone around knew that's what he had written, MidéOgema had to move from the United States.

He moved to the Garden River Reservation near St. Joseph Island in Canada. That's where I was going when I met the Windigo [Evil Spirit]. Eventually they moved to a resort called Five Rivers in Canada. But I'm way ahead of my story. . . .

The Wigwam

When I was still a young girl, MidéOgema and Minissing Odahnikwe lived in a small clapboard cottage, which was something special for an Indian community back then. But at the back of their property was the place I was really drawn to. Built way back in the woods was the most beautiful wigwam that I had ever seen. It was very large, and the doorway to it was lovely, made of heavy blankets hung so that you parted them like curtains to go in. The blankets were bright, and I loved the patterns on them.

This wigwam was very high, with a fire pit in the middle and places to sit and sleep along the sides. At the far end, in the east,

2. Good Hart is an old Odawa village located north of Little Traverse Bay.

hung a white owl. It was a snowy owl suspended from a cord of milkweed. The cord was so thin that the owl seemed to sway and swoop whenever you opened the door and the stirring of the blankets caused the air to move. Of course, when I discovered this phenomena, I couldn't resist whipping the blankets back and forth to make him fly.

As you went in the door, which was set in the western wall, ranged along the sides and back were built up long platforms about a foot off the ground. There was a second step above the first platform that could be used as a table or a bed. Finally, there was another step on top, which could hold things. The first step could be used as a step to step up to the table or as a seat to face the fire.

My second favorite part of MidéOgema's wigwam was that it was filled with amber sunlight during the day and radiated the same light at night, when the fire was lit. The roof of this wigwam was made of clear rawhide, and I have never seen anything done this way before or since. I don't know how they did it, but the rawhide was curved over the area where the owl hung, and came down lower on that side, so that the owl was illuminated during the day by the big curved window made of sunlight colors. The walls/ceiling behind the bunks, and the part of the east wall that was not rawhide, were covered with birchbark, and either side of the door was covered with elm bark. The rawhide window shining on the owl was formed the same way the roof was, but rather than a door for people it was a door for light. It was amazing.

Although it sometimes made for trouble in my life, I also was fortunate to have the examples of my grandfathers to live by. MidéOgema walked his talk, and people knew this. When he taught about the belonging of all Life to the same Cycle, people listened, myself included.

On the many walks that MidéOgema and I shared, he would always stop to take JoBash, the little snail, out of the path. He would put his finger down and make little noises, and the snail crawled up his finger. He then explained to JoBash that he needed to move him away from the trail for his own safety. Then he told

JoBash, trillium, and dragonfly by Keewaydinoquay—on muslin cloth

me to put JoBash far enough away so that he wouldn't be stepped on yet close enough so that he could get back in a day.

MidéOgema always was looking after others, from tiny JoBash to anyone who needed help in the community. I tell you this so that you will have an idea of how protective he was of those in need.

(As told to Lee Boisvert circa 1988)

The Caterpillar Man

Once I was sent to take something, I don't remember what, to some people in need who lived far away, at least for my young legs. On the way home, I came upon a man in the woods who was acting very odd. He frightened me, so I hid. I wanted to see what was wrong so I could tell my Mishomis, but I didn't want this strange man to see me.

He was going along the same path I was on, but he moved so strangely. He was jerking as he dragged himself along, as if he were a puppet and someone was pulling the strings, causing his body to jump and then bang into a tree. He would try to balance himself and take another step or two, and then—zing!—he would bang into another tree!

I couldn't tell what was wrong, but he didn't seem capable of casting any spells, so I walked up to him and asked, "Sir, can I help you?" Even though I couldn't tell what was wrong, I could see and smell that he wasn't drunk, even though he acted like it in a way. His face up close looked really ill, with deep lines, and his eyes seemed to be unseeing. I asked him several times if I could help, but he couldn't seem to speak. I did think that he was aware that someone was there with him, but he really scared me, and I didn't know how to help, so I ran home.

I went straight to MidéOgema's lodge and called out "Are you at home?"

He replied, "Bindige" [Come in], so I ran in and said, "Come quick! There's a man in the woods, and he's terribly ill!" Midé-Ogema began preparing to go help, just as he always did. While he was gathering his things together, he asked what I had seen.

And when I told him, he asked, "Does this man have his hair braided down on one side and wound up on the side of his head on the other?"

And when I said yes he said, "Well, it's about time. I am glad that he is not getting away with things anymore. I don't want you to go anywhere near this man. Do not go back to him. For a long time, this man has been cruel to people, and he deserves whatever is happening to him. He has done bad things to people, and you must stay away from him."

"But he needs help, Ni Mishomis!" I cried.

"No," he replied, "This man deserves what has come to him."

I could not believe that MidéOgema would not help this man. I had been taught to help everyone, especially by MidéOgema. I was so sure that I should help that I did not listen to him and ran back to the woods to find the man.

By this time, he had gotten worse and was frothing at the mouth, as if he had rabies, and he was snarling like an animal. There was no sign of awareness of me this time that I could see. He was so much worse that I became more frightened than before, but at least he was doing something different that I could describe.

So I ran back to MidéOgema and called out, and he said "Miinwaa!" [Come in again!].

I went in and said, "He's a lot worse than before!"

MidéOgema stood up and said, "You disobeyed me!"

"Enh, but he's desperate!" I said.

And MidéOgema said, "Yes, so he is."

"Then he needs our help!"

And then he sat down and held his arm out to me and said, "Come here and I will tell you why he is behaving as he is and why I am making this choice."

He told me how this man began his life as a young healer, very skilled and capable. And, because he was, many people knew about him far and wide and came to him for help. Then he began to use his position and skills for himself instead of just for others. I wasn't sure that was so bad, but MidéOgema explained that he took big gifts or made people promise big gifts as payment instead of them being given out of the gratitude of people's hearts. This man also used his position to harm many women, and it was thought that he killed several children, and it is known that he poisoned several adversaries. Because of this, he became known as a bad man. Instead of the light working through him, it was the darkness working through him.

"Many of us wondered how he got away with this for so long. Now you understand that he's only getting what he has coming to him. If I went to help him, I would be interfering with the Blessed Spirits."

But I still wasn't convinced, so I ran to my Nokomis (Grandmother) and asked her for help.

She said, "You must mind what MidéOgema says, for he knows about these things. That's why people come to see him all the time. He is right. This man is a very bad person, and you must stay away from him."

When MidéOgema came home for supper that night, she talked to him about this, wondering if I wasn't too young to be telling these kind of things to.

But he replied, "If she's going to be in the business of healing, she's got to know these kinds of things, and I don't think her parents have told her about them."

The next day I went down the lane to get the mail, and there was an advertisement about a boxcar full of shoes coming into the next town and that they would be sold first come first serve.

MidéOgema said, "Zhatay [my nickname] will be going to school in the fall, so she should have a good pair of shoes."

Nokomis said, "Oh?"

"Enh," said MidéOgema, "so tomorrow we will go get her some."

The next day, we got all dressed up to go to town, even though I couldn't understand why MidéOgema was interested in my clothes all of a sudden. But we started out for town. About halfway there, two men came from the woods carrying a homemade stretcher covered with a blanket.

Ni Mishomis said something fast to the two men, and they said "Gahween! No!" So Mishomis sent me some distance away, and he talked to them. Then the men set the stretcher down and walked away.

Mishomis called me back, and said to me, "I want to show you something, and I want you to remember this as long as you live, because this is what happens to people who misuse the gifts of healing."

And he was quite right. I never would forget it. He pulled the blanket back, and the man looked like his guts and flesh had been sucked out. All that was left of his head was a little knob, and his feet were little bumps and his hands were like fins. He looked as if you touched him, he would fall apart. He looked for all the world like the shed skin of a caterpillar.

"You will always remember this?"

"Enh," I replied.

Then he called to the men to come take the body away. He took me by the hand and said, "You have to know this. The temptation to misuse them comes to everyone who has been given gifts to share."

Then he turned around and walked to Nokomis's house. I was very disappointed and asked if we couldn't go on to town, but he said, "No, I think we found what we were looking for." I looked down at my feet, but he probably knew that when the men got to town there would be too much furor to accomplish anything. No one ever found out who killed that man.

But he was right . . . I never forgot. It caused me to look at the whole healing business in a different way. I was never taught these things by Nodjimahkwe, my Herb Mother, but when I told her what MidéOgema had done she approved. I also wondered if Nodjimahkwe could be like that man and worried for quite a while about it. I also began to wonder if I wanted to be in the healing business if things could end up this way! Later on I found out that there are people like this in all walks of life and that betraying one's talents can happen to anyone.

(As told to Lee Boisvert circa 1990)

"Dear Grandfathers"

*Keewaydinoquay Recalls Her Grandfathers and
Their Participation in the First Fruits Celebration of Her Early Life*

It was the Most Important Day of My Life or so I thought then. It was important. It was my Feast of First Fruits,[3] and I was to serve the entire feast of foods I had prepared myself. More exciting than that, however, was the fact that my two Most Favorite People in the Whole Wide World were BOTH going to be present: my two grandfathers.

Grandfather Moorhouse, who was called Grandfather Sauganash by the family in America, was unqualifiedly the champion storyteller of the universe. You should hear what he could do with the stories from the little black book without any pictures! They became wide-screen Panavision, although none of us had ever seen a movie then. No, he was better than that! The listeners

---

3. The Feast of the First Fruits is a traditional Anishinaabeg ceremony that celebrates the time in a young girl's life when she is introduced to the extended family, and the community, as one who is becoming a young woman, one who can contribute substantially to the ongoing of The People. In addition to a giveaway, all the food served to the guests is prepared and served by the young woman.

became participants; they identified. The Lion of Judah roared behind Mother's lilac bush, Joseph was sold into slavery from the toolshed, Daniel's lions roared in the well pit, and the quarrelsome gulls became the sweet descent of the Holy Spirit. Father said the prim, prissy, Victorian gentlemen of the town congregation would lick their lips as he dressed Judith for her encounter with Holferness. One poor abused woman in a country parish was said to have stood up and cheered as Judith drove the dagger home! But it was always the Sword of the Lord that conquered. Grandfather made people believe that could happen in their own lives, too. He ended everything with "Blessed be the Name of the Lord," even in casual conversations.

Ni Mishomis MidéOgema ran him a close second, but he was only the champion storyteller of the Whole World. He had, in fact, been declared so by an intertribal conclave of Anishinaabeg, so my father boasted, back in the days before the Grand River Bands began to think that traders and priests knew more than medicine men. I loved him devotedly because he took the time to show me many marvelously wonderful things, like the tiny footsteps of the MayWayDayKweg [spirits of moving/falling/splashing water] where they dance above the rapids, the "happy spot" on the back of a hare's head, and how to call and hold a dragonfly. He could speak the language of any bird alive, he could, and that of many four-legged animals. We clung to each other with a kind of desperate longing, MidéOgema and I, especially in those earlier days, and I never understood exactly what it was, not until I became a hexagenarian. It was that hope of hope that flows between kindred spirits and had little to do with our being related by blood.

Mother worried about my First Fruits Feast. (Now, when I think about it, I'm surprised she let me have one at all. It was distinctly an Indian celebration. Although she was genetically part Indian, she was culturally British, and there were so many Indian things of which she did NOT approve. She certainly was energetically promoting that one.) She worried about the weather. She worried about the dishes. She worried if I would make a mistake. She worried that the grandfathers might somehow dissent when they came together.

"Keep them laughing and joking," she told my father. "Keep the conversation moving. No politics, white or red. No religion. Especially no religion. Walks-With-Bears and I will keep them busy with food. That ought to do it." (At the time of the First Fruits Feast described, I was, of course, still called by my childhood name, Walks-With-Bears.)

Mother often worried about things that "might possibly" come about. More often they didn't than they did. "It's better to be a little prepared in case they do," she'd insist. Was Mother a chronic worrier? Was it that nagging fear that caused her to achieve so much? I don't know; I had a child's mind then. (In the end, it was "external" social and political pressures that caused our family any deep trouble and unhappiness. Mother had projected them all. I'm sure we conducted ourselves in a better manner for having had the possibilities presented ahead of the happenings.)

For sure, *I* didn't worry about the feast. Had Mother not trained me how to cook? Was she not Sarah Goodcook, famous among whites and Indians alike for her delectable cuisine? Had people not sent even from faraway France to obtain her recipes?

Father didn't worry either. He knew the grandfathers had long ago pleasantly agreed to pleasantly disagree. He knew they would keep their word. And they did, very pleasantly indeed.

They sat in the places of honor, my grandfathers, and laughed and laughed. Their merriment made other guests feel happy, too. And I did very well. I had expected to do so. After all, I was already in my seventh summer. I should have said I did very well *until* Grandfather MidéOgema began to tell about Nanaboozhoo and how he brought the bag of winds to our islands. A new story, one that I'd never heard before! I plopped myself down at Midé-Ogema's feet and hung on everything he said. I memorized every word. I'm afraid I was so engrossed I forgot all about the duties of a hostess—the very capabilities that I was supposedly demonstrating. Mother had to remind me about bringing in the dessert. It was a pièce d'occasion all right, chocolate mocha maple mousse served in decorated birchbark cups.

As I reluctantly dragged my feet away from the storytelling and toward the springhouse where the mousse was being kept cool, Grandfather Sauganash leaned toward Grandfather Midé-Ogema.

"You know," he spoke in a confidential tone that somehow conveyed both banter and respect, "you really shouldn't fill her head with such stories."

"Living in the Land of the Great Waters, she will need to know these things," replied MidéOgema matter-of-factly, and he deftly speared a lonely dumpling in the gravy pot.

"But she will not always live here," said Grandfather Sauganash. "Her real home is in the great stone house of this dodem [clan]." He tapped the massive silver ring on the middle finger of his right hand. On its face was a strange bird called "pelican," [which was] feeding little ones of its own kind with blood from its breast. There were also some foreign words, which read VIRTUS SEMPER VIRIDIS [Always Faithful].

MidéOgema flicked the Ajiijaak [crane] pendant on his broad chest. It was beaded in four dimensions, Slave Lake style [a style of woodland beading], and the Great Crane seemed to flap his wings in the waning light. "She has another dodem, Oonibwaakim [One who is wise]." His voice was half banter, too—also half gravy and dumpling.

My father presented each of the grandfathers with gifts of [the softest] brain-tanned leather. Mother brought out great piles of her beautiful baskets, and she and I distributed [them] to all the guests present. Our good and only neighbor, Pearse Quirck, (who was Métis [part Indian and part white] but blood brother to my Odawa grandfather by means of the Midéwewin) had practiced me to say a little speech about appreciation of and duties to my elders. I dutifully recited it in English and Anishinaabemowin. Then the grandfathers exchanged soft Canadian blankets and everybody sang "KiMinoWe-Giizhigaad" [To Your Happy Day] with great gusto.

That night, since we had so many guests, I slept between my

parents. Snuggled in the warmth, I felt like a cherished nucleus. We were very tired, but waves of gladness swept from them to me, from me to them, from our family out to all Beings everywhere. Vaguely I wished for fantastic blessings upon these parents; they deserved them.

From outside by the fire, we could hear the rise and fall of voices. Pearse in his old capote and the grandfathers in their new blankets were busily settling the affairs of the Great Lakes and smoking up a storm. They were . . . good men . . . things would . . . be . . . all right. Gently I drifted away from the Happiest Day of My Life.

Dear Grandfathers, Second Part

I loved those two grandfathers of mine with dedicated admiration and to a degree of devoted adoration that would be difficult to understand in these days of fractured family relationships. It turned out they were both right. It turned out they were both wrong—as is everyone who ever has been caught in the vicissitudes of the human cycle. It was years before I came to even a partial understanding of this.

In spite of his scorn for the ways of the White Eyes, Ni Mishomis MidéOgema passed over in their House-of-Many-Windows [hospital]. They say he sang in his sleep and drummed on the metal bed and so awakened himself for the last time. He looked at the white walls, white bed, and lovely ladies in white dresses and winged hats. He grinned.

"So the black robes are right after all?" he teased. "There are white angels in paradise."

One of the white angels tinkled, "He's an old flatterer, that one."

"And don't we love it!" said another.

Then, so we heard, Grandfather turned to a slanty-eyed angel and whispered, "Get some help. Carry me outside to lie on the earth."

The black-haired angel leaned over him. "Old One . . . honored Old One, 'they' will never permit it. You might get pneumonia."

Grandfather tugged at something around his neck. The cord broke and the contents of a little leather bag, some assorted old leaves, a small shell and some earth, black muck and white sand, spilled out across the starched sheets.

"Absolutely unsanitary!" exclaimed the Boss Angel. "Clean him up immediately."

But Ni Mishomis did not hear. His spirit had walked westward, right out of the House-of-Many-Windows, westward toward the murmuring sound of the Great Waters.

(We were told this by one Willard Thomas of Ossineke—they called him Ole Stony Eye—who was a close friend to MidéOgema and the grandfather of the slanty-eyed angel. He traveled many, many miles, to bring us this story.)

Then a rather funny thing happened, if one can only look at it that way. Some traditional friends of MidéOgema who hadn't approved of his being brought to the House-of-Many-Windows in the first place, whipped into the little hospital and whisked his body off before anyone could make a move to stop them.

At that time, it seems, they were just beginning to keep vital statistics of non-Mission Indians [those who were not Christians] in that area, and the coroner was very much impressed with his own official importance. He turned the whole Garden River Reserve upside down for miles around so he could pronounce MidéOgema officially dead. But, strangely, nobody knew a single thing about it. So . . . officially MidéOgema isn't dead. In the Moon-of-Falling-Leaves [October 1987] he will be 172 years old!

The death of Grandfather Sauganash was not what might have been expected either. In spite of his trust in the clinic at the House-of-Many-Windows, he passed over right on the shores of the Great Lake he loved so much and where he had baptized so many people.

"You might as well take him home," they had said at the

House-of-Many-Windows. "There is nothing more we can do for him here."

Mother called me at the Central State Teachers College [in Mount Pleasant, Michigan] to come home. We had been expecting this; Grandfather Sauganash was ninety-seven.

It was the fastest trip home I ever had. Billy Dabandayash, whom I hadn't seen since we were kids at the Bight country school, arranged for me to ride three mail trucks. They all said they wouldn't see me if I happened to be there. Billy himself was the first driver, and, just like I really wasn't there, he never said a word all those miles. We rolled into Manton in the middle of the night, and I tried to thank him before the next lap began, but he brushed me off gruffly.

"Neversawya [Never saw you]." Then he shifted uneasily and added, "Fitsnaygood yanow tayer famlyn'all hemaydtah oladee feealgood. Shewen toverappy [It's no good, you know, to your family and all. He made the old lady feel good. She went over happy]." He blew his nose loudly. The next driver honked [and I climbed up to continue my journey home].

Auntie Lily was the only one at the house [when I arrived].

"Change your clothes," she ordered. Certainly I was adult then, but I'd spent the better part of a long childhood responding to that same order from these same older adults. It never occurred to me to ask why we would be wearing Sunday clothes to the beach. I just did what I was told.

There was bright sunshine and very little wind. Grandfather Sauganash lay on the old red sleigh robe, propped up in the warm, sunny sand. The fingers of one hand sifted sand grains while the other dabbled occasionally in the littoral laps. With a look of utter contentment on his face, he was speaking to a considerable gathering of people, who were also dressed in their Sunday best.

"Just like a regular church service," I thought. It was.

"Surely, this is one of the most beautiful places the Lord hath made," intoned Grandfather's ministerial voice. He looked out across the calm waters to where the Yahscodeg [Lights on the Water] glinted across the reef. Far away a gull cried.

He turned his head to the people. "This is holy water. Keep it that way!" His voice thundered like a Moses on Mount Sinai. I marveled to myself that he should think we had anything to do with it and then remembered guiltily the hundreds and hundreds of stones we had skipped into the water. What little I understood then. . . .

He tried to lift himself somewhat and then gave it up. "I want you all to know," he said. "I have made many mistakes in this life. God knows I am heartily sorry for them. But coming to this place and finding here a faithful wife was not one. I am grateful. It is a good place to die among good people."

(Some twenty years before this, Grandfather Sauganash had given up his last chance to return across the sea to the stone house [in England] that I had once childishly imagined to be filled with pelicans. They—whoever "they" were—had sent him money instead. He did many things with it; I don't remember them all. My aunts received some things they needed, [and] my mother got a pair of pretty shoes like she'd always wanted—and then for some reason wouldn't wear them. He gave me a real gold ring set with a delicate Persian turquoise. He bailed Squondongeezix out of jail, paid up the mortgage on the Green Valley church, and endowed the Indian camp-meeting ground. And he bought land, the same land upon which he had been living, with a high hill looking out over the Great Lake.)

Grandfather continued his last sermon: "Freedom is the Lord's greatest gift, Freedom of Action and Freedom of Spirit. I have both. Blessed be the Name of the Lord." He tried a sermonizing gesture, but his hand dropped into the water. The great silver ring, which had become more and more loose on his finger during the past months, rolled across the lake bottom.

I started to go after it, but Auntie restrained me with a loud whisper: "Hsst. It is not fitting, a thing of Mammon. Besides, you have your best clothes on." It seems we were supposed to gaze into the heavens and sing "Guide Me, Oh Thou Great Jehovah." That was Grandfather's favorite hymn. A great emotional surge of song rose up from the people gathered there, and the airborne shorebirds came wheeling to participate just like a scene from the Holy Bible.

I wasn't really into surging and wheeling. My practical, down-to-earth Anishinaabe blood was keeping an eye on the silver ring.

That is how I came to see something no one else saw. Just for a moment his eyes flipped open again and he stared at the water around his hand. Falling to my knees, I put my face close to his. He never moved, but quite clearly he said, "Christian man," and then he winked. Yes, he did! The grandiose, dignified, reverend-father-in-God, Francis Hague Moorhouse, who had just died majestically, winked at me.

It came to me then, and a sob and a laugh rose from within me at the same time: Grandfather Sauganash had staged his own passing over . . .

There was a huge repast ready, and I found that people whom I did not recognize had come from Susan Lake, Elk River, Burt Lake, Ponshewahing, Keewaydin, Alba, Waswagoning, and Onekama. Before dinner there was much weeping, many tributes, and triumphant witnessing. The menu turned out to be platters and platters of Yorkshire pudding, cases of Canadian bacon, gallons of dumplings in white gravy, bushels of cucumber salad, and a very "dispirited" trifle. That cinched it. Nobody else [but an English-man] would have thought up that menu.

The burial was an aftermath, as befitted one who believed implicitly in the supersession of the Spirit.

(Reprinted with permission from the Miniss Kitigan Drum, copyright 1987)

Greater Grandparents

Greater Grandmother Susanna

I remember many stories about my ancestors. My mother used to tell me about her great-great-grandmother Susanna of the Moorhouse family in Yorkshire, England.[4] In the mid–eighteenth century, Susanna was born into a family of seven sons. She was a deaf-

4. This is yet another Susanna.

mute, and her family didn't know what to do with her. During the time before the American Revolution, the English government was giving away "caskets"—a box with linens, sheets, and some gold pieces, like a dowry—to each Englishwoman who would go to the American colonies to be the wife of one of the settlers there. Her parents thought, "Aha, this will be just the thing for Susanna," and they signed her up.

But it turned out that when she got here the man who agreed to take her already had a wife. His wife was crippled and could do hardly anything. So he really did need Susanna, but he expected Susanna to be a second wife—in every way. She'd been reared in a gentle home and was not in for that kind of thing. The first time he tried playing games with her, she ran. She must have done a good job of running. He went after her but couldn't find her. She ran a long ways away. He never caught her and never reported anything about her, either.

So the Moorhouse family kept on sending her things, and he kept on keeping them. He didn't want to say what had really happened. Due to the ravages of disease and war, the Moorhouse family lost all their sons. So they sent somebody to find Susanna, figuring that she probably had a family by that time.

They found the man who was supposed to be her husband, but he didn't know anything about her. Finally he admitted that she'd run away from him. They might have lost her forever if she hadn't been a deaf-mute. Somebody in Montreal remembered her because she was different. It turns out that in the woods someplace, nobody knows where, she had met and become the wife of an Indian man from near Sault Sainte Marie. (Her lack of speech was not considered a detriment to her husband, to say the least!) At one point, her husband had gone to Montreal for a shipment of cattle from Denmark.

The scout for the Moorhouse family wrote and asked if they'd support a further trip to Mackinac since he had every reason to believe that he would find Susanna there. The family agreed, so he went to Mackinac on a boat and did indeed find Susanna.

She was remembered by this man in Montreal because she was good-looking and because she couldn't talk and she had made signs. The man had apparently tried talking to her, but she gave no response except a smile. He also remembered that he'd written up the bill of sale to her husband, so he knew where they lived.

Susanna and her Indian husband and four of their children went back to Yorkshire. They left three children [behind in America]. They had grown up and were members of the tribe here and had jobs and probably wouldn't have adapted as well. The return of Susanna to England reestablished the Moorhouse line, so Susanna became one of my ancestors.

Great-Grandmothers

Elizabeth and her sister, Susanna Bpgonikwe, were born in what is now known as the Leelanau Peninsula, distant relatives of one of the children left behind by Susanna, the deaf-mute. These two sisters were given as children of thirteen and fourteen to a medicine man in payment for the life of their father. They both gave birth to daughters at the same time, days apart, fathered by the same man.

Being quite young when they had their babies, one evening the girls were restless and wanted to go to a dance—a powwow. So they left the babies in the charge of some young boys. Those boys got tired of the babies squalling, and they put them on a raft and floated them on a pond. One of them drowned. Susanna and Elizabeth both claimed the living one to be the one that was their daughter, Mistequay. But when Elizabeth had the chance to marry James Pickering she agreed to leave the child with Susanna, her sister.

✸ ✸ ✸ ✸

If I ever have any extra money in my lifetime I would like to put a little memorial in the Indian cemetery for Susanna Bpgonikwe. Every so often I turn up a lead that causes me to think that some-

Gravestone of Susanna Bpgonikwe

body I meet is the grandchild of someone who was raised by Susanna Bpgonikwe.

They'll say, "You know, my grandmother, my aunt . . . up in Leelanau. . . ."

And I'll say, "A lady by the name of Susanna Bpgonikwe?"

And they'll say, "How did you know?" She raised twenty-four children, and a lot of them were kids who were washed ashore. When this land was opened for settlement, a lot of people came in homemade boats that weren't necessarily safe. So the boats would break up when the water got rough. The lucky ones made it to shore. All she'd know was that their name was Suzy Heinz and they came from Germany—things like that.

✠ ✠ ✠ ✠

[In 1997, Keewaydinoquay's long unrealized hope was fulfilled by Dan Creely Jr. He drove her to Onomini Cemetery, and they placed the memorial for Susanna, with tears of sorrow and joy and gratitude . . . all intermingled. It rests under an apple tree. Nearby are numerous graves honoring Native American veterans of the Civil War.]

The Story of Mindemoya

The way I heard it, Mindemoya was an old woman who had lived a good life—a healthy life, and like all good Anishinaabeg grandmothers she lived in turn with her sons and her daughters, helping with babies and with the meals so things would go smoothly. Then her great-grandchildren all grew up and got married and moved away and there was Mindemoya, without any grandchildren to live with or even great-grandchildren to live with.

So she spent a day in mourning, and then she looked around to see if there was anybody who needed a grandmother. And she didn't have to look very far. She found a young woman who was a widow with a bevy of little children and needed somebody to help her. So she went to see the young woman and said, "I see you have many children and your honored brave has gone into the next cycle and you obviously need help. Since I have no more grandchildren close to me, I'd like to offer to be a helper."

The young woman was very glad to have her. Mindemoya helped her do all the chores and raise those children. Then those children got married and moved away. The young woman married a widower like herself, whose children were gone. So she had a partner, but it didn't include Mindemoya.

So Mindemoya looked around, and she found someone else. And people began to look at her and say, "How long has she been here anyway?" Some people started to figure it out; everybody had some relatives or great-grandparents who'd known her and many other people before that. They'd ask her, and she'd say, "Oh yes, many, I have helped many." But that wasn't what they were really asking, of course. They wanted to figure out how old she might be. And they were kind of curious about the medicines she used.

But, according to the story, after many years, so long there was nobody left alive who could really figure out how old Mindemoya was, that tough little body of hers did start to wear out, and eventually she did die. Of course, there were so many people from all over who should have been at her funeral, they started to worry about how they would handle this. Because if *all the people* who ought to come came they wouldn't be able to feed them. Mindemoya had never been very rich. Any money she did earn had just been put back into the family she was with, so there wasn't much to put into funerary gifts. So they decided they wouldn't announce it, that perhaps she had lived so long that a lot of people would have forgotten.

In the meantime, they did do the niceties. She did pass over, and she did travel the road to Epingishmook [Land of the West] and there was met by all the people who had seen what she'd done. They did her much honor because after all it was their great-great-grandchildren whom she'd been helping.

They said, "You've done so much and you've worked so awfully hard and you kept your patience so well that you can have almost any kind of an honor that you want. We're sorry that the people on Earth didn't see fit to do it, but we know, we see more than they do. Just say it and you can have it."

She said, "Well, could I have just a little time to think about it?"

"Yes," they said, "but you'll have to sit over there. And watch out, you can't come across the edge of the circle. You'll have to think about it, and we'll see what can be worked out."

So she sat there for a time, and nobody knows how long because there wasn't any way of measuring it. Finally she said, "I've thought it through. You did say I could have anything I want?"

They said, "Yes, [though] of course here there are things within reason, too, just like there are on Earth. But don't be afraid to ask, anyhow."

"Well," she said, "the thing that has given me the greatest joy is to help some little child who is without a mama or some-body to look after him when he's in trouble; to hold him in my arms and croon him to sleep is one of the greatest joys I've known. And since there isn't anybody on the Earthplace that's permanently appointed to be Mindemoya I ask if I could go back to Earth and be Mindemoya to the little ones who don't have anybody."

They said, "You don't have to do that anymore. You've done lots more than your share."

"But," she said, "I can have whatever I'd like, and this is what I'd like."

So it's said that whenever there's a young mother who's overly weighed down by the duties of motherhood, of keeping things going, Mindemoya appears to help her. And if there are children who've been abandoned and need a mother it's Mindemoya who comes to comfort and guide the little ones.

More Ancestors

I was taught as a child about my great-grandfather, who was the Scotsman that they found floating between Woman's Island and Whiskey Island. They thought he was dead and wanted to leave the body there, but Cecilia Manidu wouldn't let them, even though they had a canoe load of dried fish and it was packed full.

You see, in those days different work crews did different jobs. For example, young, fertile couples were sent to Amikogenda Island to tend the gardens, which were already laid out. This made sense in many ways. One is that most of the work was already done, so the newlyweds had time to spend with each other. It also probably had something to do with fertility, for everything and everyone involved. The survival of the village depended on everyone contributing what they could.

It was important that the fishing crew, whom everyone was relying on, return to Kitiganing Island with their heavy load of fish for the winter, so they were in a hurry and didn't want to stop. After some discussion, Cecilia insisted, so they did pick the body up out of the water and then left it and her on the beach some distance from the village.

After they dropped off their load of fish, they went back to pick up Cecilia and bury the body. But to their surprise both Cecilia and this strange, light-colored man were alive and well! So they took both of them home. His name was Jamie [James] Moray, and he later married the woman who had saved him.

This Scotsman proved to be a valuable member of this community because of his ability to dicker for the best bargain for himself and his village. The village sold fish and wood to steamships and sometimes huge mukukuk [birchbark boxes] of maple sugar and also wauwaushkesh wiiyaas [venison].

Eventually, Jamie began to feel quite at home with his new people and asked to join the Midéwewin. When they told him no, he asked, "Why not?"—being a bold man. "I'm good enough to marry one of your women and to work alongside you. I'm good enough to bargain and get the best deals for you. Why not?"

They said to him, "Because you have no clan."

That was the wrong thing to say to a Scotsman. Jamie Moray grew red in the face and said, "What, no clan? You are wr-r-r-ong about that!" Then he told them about his Scottish clan. They had never heard of such a thing, and they wondered if his clan had a spiritual guardian. And he said, "Our clan is that of the Mere People."

✳ ✳ ✳ ✳

Many years ago, there were many more Anishinaabe clans than are known of today. I have seen dodem markings in cemeteries carved on very old trees that include the Mere Clan, the North Star, Giant Water Bug, and a Turtle with what appears to be a book over its head.

So when Jamie explained he was of Mere Clan—the People of the Water—they were happy to take him in to their society.

✳ ✳ ✳ ✳

As an adult, I was able to visit Scotland. On this trip, I hoped to learn about the Mere Clan aspect of my heritage. So I went hunting for someone who could tell me more, but everyone kept telling me they had never heard of a Mere Clan.

The Mere Clan pin

They showed me the Moray tartan and a big pin to hold the scarf up, but it wasn't right. But they told me to come back another day when a man who knew about such things would be in.

My father had kept some of the tartan that his mother got from her father, and since cloth was so scarce it was used by my mother to make many different things, including clothes for a little girl. This is why I clearly remembered what my family tartan should look like.

When I went back to that store to talk to the man, he said, "It's not the Morays of the Firth you'll be wanting, it's the Morays of Argyle." And it was. He went into a back room and brought out some plaids, and there it was! When I pointed to it, he said, "That's the hunting tartan of the Argyle Morays!"

Then they thought I would buy a whole outfit, which was something I couldn't buy even one piece of, to my great disappointment and theirs. It was *very* expensive.

But I was able to afford the pin of the Moray clan, and it has a mermaid on it. I was so excited to see it because it shows the Mere Clan connection!

Jamie Moray lived on that island for quite a few years. Then one day he received a letter from the family doctor back in Scotland telling him that his father was dying and wanted to see him and that he had better hurry. So Jamie sailed back to Scotland and did get to see his father. But on the way back to America James himself became ill and died of cholera before he made it home.

His wife, Cecilia Manidu, remained on Kitiganing Island and is buried there.

(As told to Lee Boisvert circa 1992)

Trying to Belong

As a Young Child

Churches

Every morning my mother read to me from the Bible, and every night my father took me to the top of the hill and we sang prayers. They had agreed between themselves that if they had children they would allow them to make their own choices. And they fulfilled this promise, even though I ended up being all the children they could have.

Early in life I developed a keen interest in religious studies. Having grandfathers who were spiritual leaders in their communities may have fostered my fascination beyond that of other children my age. But I kept running into difficulties.

My first disappointment came when I wasn't allowed to go to drum classes with the boys. MidéOgema had even spoken up for me, but that still didn't change things. The boys were taught how to drum. They were even taught how to make them!

I showed up at the first drumming class, hoping to be included, but every time I tried to pick up a beater someone would quietly take it out of my hand. I was furious!

When I went to MidéOgema, he said to me, "With the Blessed Ones, there is no sex. Sex is merely an ornament in this planetary life cycle. A really nice decoration but only an ornament, nevertheless. What is important is to walk your life on the sacred path."

Giving up, I did sit outside and listen every time I had a

chance. That's how I know today whether our people are drumming properly or not.

So then I decided to try other ways of looking at spirituality, which made my mother very happy.

I took great pride and excelled in the class work required for the Roman Catholic catechism (my Episcopalian grandfather insisted that we put the *Roman* in front of *Catholic*). Perhaps on some level I hoped that this would help me fit into a community that never warmed up to me because of my mixed-blood heritage.

I was excited and eagerly looked forward to the ceremony for my First Communion. While waiting to be fitted for my white gown and white shoes, the priest came by to congratulate the line of students.

As he paused in front of me, a nun looked up from her work and said, "Father, she is not one of us, she is one of them." It wasn't because I was Indian but because my Grandfather was MidéOgema.

The hurt that we receive from people we hold in esteem and honor can be the worst of all. No child should have to experience this, especially from leaders of the church. My visions of a white gown and shoes dissolved along with my hope for acceptance. I left outcast, alone, and never went back to the "church of the whites."

(As told to Rich Maples circa 1990)

Friends had told me I should come to the Pentecostal church. This church had both white and Native people in the congregation. This blend of people made me more comfortable. I rededicated myself to my studies. I especially enjoyed the singing. They would sing bass and soprano and alto, and soon everyone would be swaying and clapping and singing along.

One service, the minister asked if there were any requests for a favorite song. I raised my hand very enthusiastically and was asked what song I would like to hear. I responded, "The Bear Song." The puzzled preacher said that he couldn't think of any bear song and asked what bear song I was thinking of. "Oh yes," I said,

"Gladly, the Cross-Eyed Bear." You see, I had thought the song was about a bear named Gladly who was cross-eyed.

The congregation exploded into laughter. Tears rolled down cheeks as people tried to regain their composure, only to lose it again. I wasn't sure what I had said but again felt outcast and humiliated. I couldn't bear to return to this church, either. I was embarrassed and felt totally isolated, thinking that I didn't belong anywhere. [Many children misunderstand the words of hymns, but not all take it as seriously as little Zhatay did.]

(As told to Rich Maples circa 1990)

Vision Quest

Adult Naming

The problem for me was that I was neither here nor there. The only one who noticed there was something wrong for me was Pearse.

He'd had a wife and a daughter, and his wife had died in childbirth. His wife and little girl were buried in the yard next to his cabin. He lived alone there about two miles away.

I remember I was sitting in my place up on the dunes soon after they took Val, and along comes Pearse. I know now that he knew that I went there.

He said, "Why, Zhatay, what's the matter? It looks like you've been crying."

I said, "No, I haven't."

And he said, "Well, it's not raining."

He finally got me to [talk about it], and I said, "All the kids I know, they all belong to something. But I don't belong here, and I don't belong there, and I don't belong anywhere."

He said, "Well, you certainly do. Your grandfather was a very famous man. You can speak his name anywhere in the state of Michigan and every Indian knows who he is. Not that they'd all agree with him, but they all know who he is. And you belong in the Midéwewin."[1]

---

1. The Midéwewin, or Grand Medicine Society, fosters and preserves another form of spiritual practice of Anishinaabeg People. It is also called the Midéwin and Midé.

And I said, "Do you belong to the Midéwewin?"

He said, "Well, yes, I do, but that's not the reason I was telling you that you ought to [join this society]. I was just saying that your family does belong there, and their granddaughter belongs there, too."

So he talked to my parents [about my need to belong and about sending me out on a vision quest]. But neither of my parents was willing to do anything about it.

Pearse said, "Well, if I stand with her, will you permit that?"

And they said, "If you would be her sponsor, we would feel honored. It would be good to know that you were her sponsor."

So that man, who at the time seemed to me like an old man, paddled me across the Grand Traverse West Bay and East Bay along the shore near Acme and all the way up past Good Hart and past Little Traverse Bay, where Petoskey sits now, and all the way along Waugoshance Point to someplace near where Mackinaw City is now. There was a point they used to call Ghost Point, where they were having a big ceremony for young people coming of age. This was the first time they had had one for girls in ten years.

$$ \text{※ ※ ※ ※} $$

It was still illegal.[2] The first thing they [the elders] greeted us with was what to do in case the police came. They said they would beat on the drum and we should all run into the woods and not come back to camp at all and slowly make our way back to where we came from.

They had different [fasting sites for us each to stay in already] picked out. Instead of having people go out and pick sites of their own, they had put numbers on them. We were supposed to go out and see what site appealed to us and come back and say what number the site was. By the time we got there, most of the sites had been taken, and the ones left were the least desirable.

2. In 1978, the American Indian Religious Freedom Act was enacted. Before that time, Native religious and spiritual practices were forbidden by law.

I only saw two animals at my fasting site. Somehow I had gotten the idea that you had to see an animal . . . that that was the way it worked—and then that animal is your guardian. And the two animals I saw were crayfish, little lobsterlike things, and some big fat June bugs. They were coming out of their pupae cases and leaving them on the shore. I thought I'd just as soon die as be called "Big Fat June Bug."

The site I got was on a little gravel spit that went out into the lake. They gave us a few sticks and a blanket. We were supposed to put the sticks up and put the blanket over it. We weren't supposed to talk to anybody. So I sat in my little shelter. And all the time I was afraid that I would be called Big Fat June Bug or Fighting Crayfish for the rest of my life. There was a man who was supposed to come around and see that we were all right. We weren't supposed to talk back to him, and he kept saying to me, "You're not supposed to wrap yourself in that blanket. You're supposed to sit in a little house made with it."

Well, I knew that, but every time I put the blanket around these sticks the wind would blow it down again. I remember he had a funny squeaky voice, and I couldn't imagine what was wrong with him. (As I realized later, what appeared to me as a young girl to be an adult male was actually an older boy or a fairly young man.)

When that part [fasting alone for days] was over, we were supposed to talk with a committee of elders. As far as I was concerned, if Pearse had not been there I would have run. Fisher Crab or Big Fat June Bug . . . I didn't want to be either one of them. I was too embarrassed; I couldn't run.

When it came time to interview these elders, I said to Pearse, "I don't want to do this."

He said, "I don't suppose you do, but you have to be brave. This is a part of it and what you're supposed to do."

I said, "Do I have to tell them everything that happened?"

He said, "Everything."

I said, "I don't want to tell them everything."

He said, "That has nothing to do with it; you still have to tell them." So I told them about how I didn't want to be named after a big fat June bug.

They asked me about my fasting site tent blowing down, and I said, "Yes, it was just awful. I couldn't keep it up. The wind kept blowing it down one time after the other."

They said to me, "Is that so? How many times? More than seven?"

And I said, "Oh, yeah, seven anyhow, maybe more. The man with the squeaky voice, he'll tell you that's the truth."

We continued the ceremony. We had a sweat. There must have been fifteen other girls there. I was terribly embarrassed. I went into this sweat lodge, covering myself with my arms, thinking, "What are all these old ladies doing here?" Some of them must have been sixteen years old, at least. I suppose they were looking at me wondering what this little girl was doing there. But I wouldn't have been there if I hadn't been mature. That was one of the requirements in those days.[3]

But, anyhow, when it came to the family I probably would have quit and run again if it wasn't that Pearse was there, standing beside me. And I had made my own outfit. That was another requirement. You had to make your own moccasins and headband. And I thought what I made was utterly lovely, but compared to the ones next to me mine must have been utterly awful. Theirs had lovely, shiny, sparkly, colored beads, while my beads were made out of wood. My dad had made them, one at a time.

But when we got up there and they gave me my name, all of that other junk just rolled away by the wayside because they didn't call me Big Fat June Bug. They named me Keewaydinoquay [Woman-of-The-Northwest-Wind], after that wind I sat in for three days. And I was glad. I was very glad. I had no idea of any overtones or connotations or forecastings or anything like that; it was just that I had a nice name. I finally belonged somewhere, and there were a lot of people that I belonged to.

We had stopped on the way up at a couple of camps, so on the

3. By "mature," Keewaydinoquay means having come of age and begun menses.

Headband made by young Walks-With-Bears for her Vision Quest, using beads made by her father

way back we did also. People would say to Pearse, "Does the young lady have her name?"

And he would say, "Yes."

And they would say, "And might we be permitted to know what it is? Because some people don't like to tell their names, you know."

And he would say, "Oh, I don't think she'd mind." He'd look at me to say it. I could tell, from the way they acted, that they thought this was a good name, but I didn't know why.

Then, when we got all the way home, of course this was the first thing my parents asked. And when I told them my new name was Keewaydinoquay they also liked the name. For some reason, I had expected them to dislike it, but they both did like it. That helped a great deal. I know my mom didn't send me off with gifts for the elders and food for the feast. The only thing I can think of is Pearse must have taken care of all those things for me.

$$\text{※ ※ ※ ※}$$

[Soon afterward] we moved away from there, and I never saw Pearse again. When I did go back as a young woman to Pearse's place, it was abandoned. I felt so badly about it [that] my dad went back there with me. He thought if [Pearse] had died of a heart attack or something maybe he could help find the body. He was a big man . . . over six feet tall.

$$\text{※ ※ ※ ※}$$

When I told my teacher at school my new name [Keewaydino-quay], she said, "Doesn't anybody in your family ever have a decent Christian name?"

136

I said, "Yes, my grandmother did."

She said, "Good, what was that?" I said, "Margaret."

She said, "Fine, that's what we'll put down for you." She wrote down Margaret Cook. And I got the impression she thought she was doing me a favor. Later on I had to go to high school under that name, and when I wanted to graduate under my right name they said, no, I had to take it under the name that earned it.

And when I went to college they told me I'd have to do high school all over again if I wanted to change it. When it came time to work on my doctorate, people asked me where I would go to school in ethnobotany [the study of plants as they are used by ethnic groups].

I said, "The first university that tells me I can have my graduation certificate printed with my right name on it is the one I'll go to." The first one to agree to that was the University of Michigan, and that's why I went there.

Apprenticeship with Nodjimahkwe

The traditional thing after a vision quest was to become an apprentice.

I was the one who wanted to be apprenticed. It was part of belonging somewhere. And I wanted to belong. Above all things, I wanted to belong. I think it was just as much by elimination as by choice that I wound up with Nodjimahkwe.

She was my Herb Mother. She was the woman to whom I was apprenticed when I first became a woman. It used to be, a long time ago, that anybody of adult status, or near adult status, would be apprenticed out to somebody who was recognized as doing something very, very, very well within the village or the band or the tribe. This skill was something they were expected to share with everybody. It was usually based on some talent that the person had shown when they were little. It also was often based upon one's Birth Portent.[1]

My parents couldn't agree on a choice.

I kind of liked beadwork. But I wasn't quite good enough for that. And, besides, my mother didn't approve, morally, of the

---

1. "The Anishinaabeg have no such thing as astrology. It is believed, however, that occurrences in the natural world at the time of a person's birth do give some indication of innate qualities which he may develop to his benefit as the personality matures" (Keewaydinoquay *Min,* 3). Birth Portents are based on the moon one is born in. There are thirteen moons in a year.

people who did the best beadwork in the village at that time. But both my parents loved plants, just loved plants. My mother had huge gardens. People came from all over to look at them. She preserved all kinds of things—canning and drying. Almost everything that we ate she grew. She also planted all kinds of flowers, and my dad was nuts about trees. My parents both approved of what she [Nodjimahkwe] had to teach. And they both approved of Nodjimahkwe because her character was far above reproach.

She was an old lady. But she could run like crazy, so she can't have been so old! She had some wrinkles. Not so many. But from where I was she was an old lady. In her mid-forties maybe?

My mama made a bag and decorated it and put kinnikinnick in it. The bag was made of deerskin because cloth was so scarce. [This bag was intended as a petition for me to become her apprentice.]

米 米 米 米

I remember that then my Aunt Lily told me a story about the Methodists and cloth. I was looking at a picture of the members of the Methodist church, and I noticed that they were all men. When I commented on this, she explained that the Methodists and Catholics had quite a competition to attract the most members from the Indian community. People loved the Methodist meetings because of the singing. But, even though the men joined, the women wouldn't come and be saved.

It took some time before the Methodist missionaries were able to understand what the problem was. You see, one of the jobs of the missionaries was to get their womenfolk to teach Indian women about the "proper" way to deal with their menstrual time. The Methodists had decreed that the traditional way of using sphagnum moss was unsanitary and that the Indian women needed to make sanitary pads out of cloth. Since the women didn't have cloth, the missionaries gave them some. But the women were not about to waste it on their moon flow! It was too rare. Instead, they used it for baby clothes and special occasions. As it turns out, use of the moss is far more sanitary, but the Methodists did not approve of any menstrual blood showing at all.[2]

So the Methodists thought the women were taking cloth under false pretenses. They almost lost a chance to convert the Indians because they didn't understand until someone explained it to them.

(As told to Lee Boisvert circa 1994)

✳ ✳ ✳ ✳

I took the beautifully beaded bag to Nodjimahkwe. I suppose that my folks had been to see Nodjimahkwe two or three times before I went, but they didn't tell me that. I learned what I was supposed to say in English and Anishinaabemowin. And Pearse coached me in how to say it properly.

This was the first time I ever heard the term *Grandmother* being used for a revered elder person not blood related.

I remember [that] the petition he taught me began: "Revered Grandmother of The People," and I said, "But she's not my grandmother."

"But," he said, "she is truly your Grandmother, for she is a knowledgeable leader of The People, and the welfare of The People is the first concern of her mind and heart."

The formal asking continued: "I come as a true daughter of the Crane, asking you to accept this petition bag for apprenticeship in learning good medicines. And I promise that whatever I learn shall be used only for the welfare of The People."

It has to be sixty-five years since I said that. . . . That shows how important it was. I practiced and practiced and practiced. And if she had talked with anybody else previously she didn't let on. I was very happy, and she was very happy. And in my youthful callowness I thought she ought to be happy to have an apprentice like me. I didn't realize the enormity of what she'd given me until I needed it for my own family.

2. Sphagnum moss is well suited for use as a menstrual pad. It is absorbent and antibacterial. It also was used as a diaper since it is renewable and completely biodegradable.

It had been a long time since she'd had an apprentice. She was so happy she actually cried a little bit. I thought that was strange.

I asked my mother about it, and my mother said, "Sometimes people cry for gladness as well as sadness."

I said, "I didn't know that. I thought they laughed for gladness."

She said, "Sometimes laughter is for sadness, too. You can hear the sadness in it."

And I said, "I hadn't noticed that. Next time you hear a sad laugh, let me know."

Nodjimahkwe was, indeed, everything my parents hoped she'd be. I just wish I could remember everything that I ever heard from her. I worked with her off and on for a long time but officially for four years. Then, due to the things that happened to me, I didn't finish up my time with her. So then I went back later and finished up formally. She, again, is someone I never had a chance to really thank as much as I would like. So I'll have to do it in another way.

She was what you would wish that all the ancestors had been. She knew what she needed to do, and she knew where she was going. It was *hard* on her because she was the only healing person who was accepted in the whole county. The church groups were down on her and anybody else who practiced what they called "medicine" because they thought it was against religious principles. They wouldn't have her, you see, because she would have had to reject the Midéwewin, and she couldn't do that. If she had done that, there would have been nobody to do medicinals for the Indians.

Umh . . . it was a sad thing, that . . . it was a long time before I could understand, but now I do, and, you see, it was because of the prayers. If it was a straight plant treatment or something like that . . . the prayers were to the plant. The prayers that were used when it was administered . . . that was the pagan part that they couldn't accept. They were quite literally asking people to take their lives in their hands [if they were] to separate themselves from the plant medicines because there was no substitute for them back then.

It must have cost her a lot when it got so that all the Indians went to churches.

She missed the social life, and a lot of the ministers would say, "Don't see that woman, she's bad." Anybody who took that stand just put themselves out there like a sitting duck for all the white people to shoot at, and the white people took advantage of it like crazy. But even then I think she would have gone to church just because she wanted to be with people. She used to sing.

We could sometimes hear her singing, and she would say "I love to sing," but if she had gone to church, you see, then there wouldn't have been anybody to heal the Indians because the doctors wouldn't take Indians for any kind of treatment or drugs. They wouldn't give anything to Indians unless it was cash up front.

The Indian folk who became the first Christians in the area were thankful to her not only for accepting to live a different life on a daily basis but also [for] accepting of that which could be of help for them because there were no hospitals. Nowadays missions have hospitals connected with them, but in those days there was nothing like that.

When my mother was pregnant with me, she didn't want to go to Traverse City because they turned Indians away. There were awful stories about Indian women giving birth on the steps of the hospital. The local doctors wouldn't take you unless you paid the bill first, and then sometimes the bill would turn out to be different from what you'd paid and you'd be asked to pay more. Of course, you never got anything back.

I didn't understand for a long time, and for a part of my adult life [I] resented that they had to be so against herbals, which are an essential component of native religion. Now I understand: in order to gather plants, you have to pray over them, talk to them. But to the Christians that was praying to the plant.

They didn't realize it was really saying to the Creator: "Thanks for creating this wonderful plant and for what it can do to help us." It could have been [explained] that way, and a lot of people's heartbreaks and deaths could have been avoided. But people didn't realize that.

Nodjimahkwe started me with simple things. She showed me her house and showed me where she stored all her herbs—a wonderful place, full of books and plants. And she had all kinds of things [with which] to grind and make mixtures. It was just intriguing. [Her] mashkikiwig [medicine wigwam] was like a very long, narrow, and high log cabin, and she had an extra bin across the top of it [on which] to hang things, and shelves with all kinds of storage. The rafters were made on purpose so you could hang things [from them], too.

She had her standards, and she said that if an herbalist took the lives of the big plants she made a promise to use them in a medicinal way for the betterment of The People. She would never allow herself to rest until they were properly taken care of, so that they would be dried or ready for whatever virtue you asked the plant for.

Sometimes people would come to her with a sore or a sickness she wasn't sure how to treat. Then she would often go to a special place to sit, somewhere up high. I don't know what direction it was in. She taught me to call her, for there were a number of times when there was real need, so she taught me to stand where my voice would echo. She also taught me to flash mirrors . . . all to let her know that she was really desperately needed.

She would go off, and she would say, "Now, if it is not desperate, tell them to come back another day." She'd come back later, and the worry lines would be [gone from] her face.

Out in back, she had a tiny sweat lodge, a little bitty thing, just big enough for her. Nearby she had a spring she had grubbed out herself. Sometimes she would go into the sweat lodge after she finished working or when she needed to figure out what to do.

She would have me pass a couple of hot stones in, and she'd say, "I don't need you anymore." When she came out of the sweat, she went into the cold spring. By the next day, she would have thought out a plan.

She didn't make it difficult for people.

Instead of saying, "Well, I believe if we call the right spirits," she'd say, "What would you give for your arm to be straight again? What would you trade?"

She made it practical.

She'd make a deal . . . like she'd say, "If in three or four months it's no better than it was before, then I'll return the part I haven't eaten up. . . ."

"But," she'd say, "you have to give me something to show me that you mean it." The healing required their participation as much as her own.

I don't know where she got money to pay for things. She took all kinds of [barter] in payment, bushels of potatoes, tomatoes in tomato season, even though she had tomatoes in her own garden. She'd take what people gave her. Sometimes she got beautiful things, sometimes she'd get pecans, and sometimes she got bad things like the rubbery gooseberry jam I was given once.

You're supposed to take, with thanks, whatever anybody offers you. Once, when I was older, a family all had ringworm, and I think that one of the reasons they came out to me was that we are sort of isolated out here and they didn't have to shower. I also wasn't going to see anybody who was related to them. So we worked on it, and they gave me twelve jars of gooseberry jam.

I thought, "Wow, I like gooseberry jam!"

But it was the strangest stuff I have every seen. It was so thick and heavy that it actually bounced. It was like rubber, and you couldn't get a spoon into it. . . . You certainly couldn't spread it. I had to put it on my income tax because in order to count the money, to count the travel that I expend in doing my medicine work, I have to tell what I get back for it. I remember it just galled me to have to put down those twelve jars of gooseberry jam that they gave me.

The accountant came up to me, and I said, "These aren't worth anything." She responded "What is their value?" I said, "Absolutely nothing. In fact, it is a negative, so take off four dollars!" My accountant ended up calling the grocery store and asking what the current price for gooseberry jam was. Then she multiplied it by twelve [and used that figure], and I just resented that.

It was so bad that I got mad at it and threw a jar down. And the jar cracked, and this glop just stood there, jar shaped. I picked

144

it up and handled it, and when I threw it down it actually bounced—not really high, but it did bounce. So I set it out in the woods for the animals. I used to set out a pot if I burned something on the bottom and let the animals clean it out. That was the easiest way, you know. Out here you don't have to worry about disease. For the next two or three weeks, there were these reproachful-looking wau-w-aushkesh (deer) trying to talk with their mouths stuck shut . . . shaking their antlers at me.

✻ ✻ ✻ ✻

She'd often send me to the drugstore for something, and at first the druggist would look at me and say, "That's gonna cost," and I'd say, "Let me know how much it is you wish to see." Which to me was a recommendation, you know.

He'd say, "Indian money, just the same." But then after a while, you see, he got so that he knew that I really did have the means to pay him. It was a real victory when he made up the prescription and handed it to me without saying, "Let me see the money." I gave him the money, and I realized that he had changed his attitude.

✻ ✻ ✻ ✻

I don't know where Nodjimahkwe got the money. I don't have the foggiest notion.

✻ ✻ ✻ ✻

There were certain things Nodjimahkwe would charge people for and other things she wouldn't. She took money for medicine or for healing cuts or surgery, for stitching somebody up or taking out some foreign object, things like that. She didn't charge for the plants healing the cut, but if she stitched the cut and it took her skill to do it she would take money for it. But she wouldn't take money for prayers.

Sometimes people would pull out a small amount of money, and they'd say, "I don't suppose you'd take money for this."

And she'd say, "Which part of it? For saving the life of your only son, I will take more than that. For praying for your family so that this doesn't happen again, I will take no money."

She worked out the formula, and some people would come around after a year or so and say, "Are you still praying for our family so we'll treat the baby right?"

She would say, "Yes," and they'd say, "Do you want money?"

And she'd say, "Not for praying, but you better not let him get hurt." She thought that some people were very careless—not taking care of their children the way they should.

She was respected enough that if she walked around the village in the evening and saw a baby in the cradle and said it looked cold, the family would start a fire—in case she was in league with a spirit or something. They'd do what she said because they didn't want her to curse them. People thought she could work magic and could pull down the spirits. Of course, she could. But she also knew the plants and the ways of life and death.

There were times that she used a bowl, and she'd put it in front of the person and say, "We give thanks to the blessed plants for this healing. We give thanks to the Creator for the healing within the plants. And we give thanks that our brother can be healed."

I remember one time seeing her take a baby that was so covered with decay—open sores—that it looked like it was already gone. She took that baby in her hands like a dear little child and she had me make a bath for the baby—and put it in and out and in and out. But before she did anything at all she gave thanks that this baby was going to be healed. And it was!

She had something like a smokehouse, but it was more like a shower house. She used this for adults that had some form of contagion. She'd take pails of disinfectant and throw it over the top of her. She had a big can, and you could mix the water and the solution—because a lot of adults weren't used to the change of temperature. There were holes in the can that would [allow the solution to] trickle.

For this baby, she had me bring her two pails of water every day, and she went in there herself and poured it over herself for a whole week. She didn't tell me what was in it. I think she was sanitizing herself.

I asked her what the baby had, and she said, "It's a disease of filth. And if people keep themselves clean they don't ever have to worry about things like that." Maybe it was something like impetigo.

That week she gave her life for that child. We heated the water and soaked her clothes in vinegar and handled the baby three times a day and made baby food for the baby . . . [and medicine with elm bark]. She used Saint-John's-wort a lot. Whatever she made for the baby had a root in it. She'd put in bloodroot in case it was a fungus. She'd put St.-John's-wort on it and powdered it. She had me wear gloves and wash them in the same solution as her clothes. She let the mother take the baby home a couple of times because people, relatives, were afraid she was doing magic on it, but she insisted the mother bring the baby back.

After she finished taking care of herself, she'd go down to the lake. Then she'd have me make something for her—oatmeal or something simple.

She'd do things like splash the water in the four directions and then pour it all over herself, but she was a smart woman. She'd also follow up. . . .

If she knew she had to deliver a baby, she'd go off by herself for a few hours to order her thoughts. When we'd get to the place where things needed to be done, she'd just snap it all out: "Now you do that" and "You do this."

I was at deliveries, and I ran to get things and learned a great deal. One of the first things I did was to dam up a stream—make a little stone basin, big enough to hold a baby, to wash the newborn baby in. The first time I saw a baby born I was of no use to her at all. I just stood there. Fortunately, I had seen a calf delivered and a foal delivered of a horse and little animals, but I thought that's the way the animals do it. I didn't apply it to human beings.

She gave me a bowl to hold, and I was still there holding the bowl when it was over. I couldn't wait to get home and tell my mother about it. My mother was very upset and wanted to revoke the apprenticeship.

My father said, "Well, why? We need people to know how to do this."

They were quarreling about it, and Nodjimahkwe came and said, "I'm glad you're talking about it. I had assumed she would know. But it seems to me she ought to know, she's ripe." My mother said I could do the other training [herbal], and she'd think about the deliveries. But Nodjimahkwe went straight ahead and had me do things for the birthings.

There were some deaths she didn't let me see—some bodies. It was my job to boil all the water and sanitize all the equipment she was to use. I'd do it in the morning, and then I'd have to do it all over again at night. I'd say, "But I did all that already." And she'd say, "I want you to remember all the equipment you are to use."

Nodjimahkwe's Childhood

As Nodjimahkwe came to know and trust me, she told me stories of her own childhood and how she came to the village of Onominee, where her mother's relatives lived. She came from the area [south of] the border between Wisconsin and Michigan. There were several bands of Indians there. When she was about my age, around nine years old, she had a best girlfriend to whom she could talk about anything. As a symbol of their friendship, they each made identical beaded belt bags. Around the same time, Nodjimahkwe was apprenticed to a well-known medicine man.

He was a good medicine man as far as medicine, but he was not really good. She didn't know that at first, but she suspected some things. There were times that he didn't pay as much attention to people as he should have. He said things like, "Oh, it's not important—don't worry about that wound," when he really should have cleaned it out and cauterized it.

This same person is also the medicine man who called a number of elders together for a meeting and then fed them a certain mushroom that harmlessly causes urine to run bright red. Instead of telling the elders what he had done, he used their all too natural fright and worry to control them for his own gain.

After she had been working with him for some time, long enough to know what medicines ought to be used for, there was a local fight between two village groups about who was going to be the head of the local band. Nodjimahkwe was helping the medicine man on the battlefield. The leader of one group, Spinning-Feather, was brought in bleeding profusely. Nodjimahkwe had just happened to finish what she had to do, and she saw that her mashkiki [medicine man] was giving him medicine that causes blood to flow rapidly instead of something to coagulate the blood. When Nodjimahkwe saw what he was giving to Spinning-Feather, she sort of gasped, and he heard her and turned and looked at her and narrowed his eyes. She knew something wasn't right, but she didn't know what. [Spinning-Feather] eventually bled to death. Soon afterward the medicine man was given much honor by the rival chieftain, who annexed Spinning-Feather's village.

Nodjimahkwe ran home, extremely upset by what she had seen. She admired and had been learning a lot from this medicine man. A medicine person's duty is to heal. He was of the Midéwin, and he held the Midéwin services and rituals for all the bands in that area. She cried and cried and threw herself in her mother's arms. Indians are trained young that they are not to make fools of themselves in that sort of emotional way. But her mother knew that something terrible had happened, and she pressed her to tell what had happened. So Nodjimahkwe told her what she had seen. Her parents at first could not believe it.

"Surely you are mistaken," they said. But she was firm: "No, this is what I saw."

They looked at each other and must have discussed it among themselves because at about two o'clock in the morning her parents woke her up and said, "Get dressed, we're leaving."

She said, "Leaving? Why? But this is home."

They said, "Yes, but it is not home any longer. You told us the truth about what you saw?"

And she replied, "Yes, of course."

They said, "All right . . . this man has done something wrong, and he won't rest until he takes everybody in the family that knows it. Because he thought nothing of taking such a fine person as Spinning-Feather, he won't think anything of us. We are nobody compared to Spinning-Feather."

She said, "Oh, I shouldn't have told you."

But they assured her, "There wouldn't be much pleasure for us to live without you and your little brother, so we will go together as a family."

Nodjimahkwe asked if she couldn't at least go tell her best friend why they were leaving. But they dared not let her do it. She was never in touch with her friend again until she met the Candle-Headed Grandson.

She said she thought the reason they forced her to leave without telling her friend was that they were afraid that she would leave something or leave some signs in the sand or do something that would give an indication where they had gone, and with the power of the chief reaching out in the territory they might be followed. As an adult, it seemed logical. But as a little girl she thought the whole thing absolutely silly. She cried and cried until they finally told her that if she couldn't keep still and carry her things out to the canoe they would have to put her to sleep, as they had already done with her little brother.

They packed a few necessary things and left that night. They were afraid that as soon as it started to turn daylight the people who lived next to them would notice that there wasn't any movement around their wigwam and no morning sounds. So they had to leave her father's favorite dog, [one] that he had trained when he was little and that he had worked and hunted with and was of great value

150

to that family. Nodjimahkwe said if her father would leave that dog she should have known that it was a really serious situation. But she thought that maybe she was just too young to catch on to that. She said she didn't even know for sure that her parents knew where it was they were going. But she thinks that they did and that they didn't tell her because they didn't want it passed on.

When it got light, they pulled in at a little island, and they took the very few things that they had taken with them out of the canoe and carried them inland on this little island. Then her mother and father picked up the canoe itself and carried it inland. Then her mother and father took branches and swept the sand, starting at the edge of the lake, so that their footprints wouldn't show.

She saw that her parents were very much frightened, and she started to cry again. They told her that she would have to keep still or they would have to make her keep still.

Her father said, "It would be best if you could sleep because, only for a while, we will have to turn the days and the nights around. We will travel in the night and sleep in the day. But if you can't sleep keep very still and pray very hard." They kept the little brother asleep day and night.

Sure enough, one of their friends came three days later to the place where they were hiding and said, "You were right. He turned the place upside down trying to find her. But you'll have to move farther away. Because if I could find her he can, too. I don't know now if someone didn't see me come this way."

They were on Gull Island. Everybody in the village knew where their parents came from, and the medicine man could come and check it out. They didn't want their parents to get in trouble, either, so they finally decided to go to the village of Nodjimahkwe's maternal grandparents, which was far enough away. It was a small, rather impoverished village, where the band was not noted for political action. They had to travel by little bits because they only had a canoe. And they went at night so they wouldn't be seen by anybody. When they had to make the big lake crossing, they waited until it was really calm and smooth. That's how she happened to be in the village of Onominee.

When they got there, nearly all the people in the village had log houses. If they had wigwams, they used them for storage places or places for the kids to romp and play when the weather was bad. Nodjimahkwe's parents built a wigwam, and they told the grandmother to say that they were just building the wigwam because they had come for a final visit to the grandmother. A predeath visit. The villagers accepted that and thought that was a really nice thing for them to do.

She said for a long time her father and mother would just take the children and disappear if newcomers or outsiders showed up at the village. They didn't want to be anyplace where there might be retribution upon the people because of them. It was a long time before they built a house. In fact, the building that Nodjimahkwe used was like a little barn and had been her grandmother's house. The family couldn't change their clan because you are clan born, but her father did change his name. The mother couldn't change hers, but she did ask her mother to call her by her maiden name, her infant name, which her mother thought was awfully silly. They may not ever have told her the real reason. Maybe they were afraid she might say something in a delirium.

✻ ✻ ✻ ✻

Nodjimahkwe didn't have a medicine person [with whom] to continue her apprenticeship, so she trained by picking up on anything and everything from anybody and anywhere.

Anything that anybody remembered that they used or that they knew or somebody that came in from another village, she'd listen to them and be polite, and first thing you know she'd be over there with a present and saying, "In your village is there a medicine person?"

If they said no, she'd say, "Well, I was just wondering how you managed that sort of thing and who did it." And they'd tell her about whoever came in to do the ceremonies or whatever.

She would ask them what they remembered about that person. Sometimes they would remember silly things, like he had a very large eagle feather fan or something like that, which was not very useful to her. But sometimes they would have long stories about how their little brother was dying of a cough of some kind and he spit up blood and this man came and did this and that and he was all right.

Then she'd say, "Did you see what he did? How did he come in? What did he have in his hands? Did he give him something to drink? Did he give him something to eat? Did he give a sweat? Did he lower him into cold water?" Sometimes she'd be lucky and a person would remember in complete detail and she'd come home just floating. Then she'd rush out to the woods and get stuff needed for that healing.

Nodjimahkwe was a very educated woman. She was not just a ritualist, an herbalist, not just a doctor of herbal medicine. She knew how to work with people. She was a practical psychologist.

The Candle-Headed Man

One of the most dramatic healings I ever saw Nodjimahkwe perform was on the Candle-Headed Man. I was about eleven or twelve, about two and a half years into my apprenticeship. One night she had just come back from the hills, where she had gathered herbs and put them in her mashkikiweg (wigwam for medicines). The night was growing late, and she was walking back to her house with the light of a large torch. She was just thinking to herself that there was so much moonlight she should put the torch out . . . that she didn't really need it, when something whizzed through the air and landed at her feet.

She was surprised and knelt down to see what it was. It was a beaded bag. When she picked it up, she thought it was her own beaded bag, but when she looked closer she saw that it wasn't hers, and then she was afraid.

Then she heard a voice that was very muffled say, "Not to frighten you, medicine woman, but I have come many miles and walked many years to find you. Do you recognize this bag?"

She looked at the bag again and said, "Yes, this bag was made by my blood sister." Then she thought that the political net had perhaps at last wound tight around her, and she demanded that the person show himself.

When he refused to do so, she was more afraid. But then he told her that he looked so bad and that she was his last hope. By now he was in such a state that he was afraid to have her look.

She said, "Well, I can't help you unless you let me see."

He said, "First I must tell you things that my grandmother told me."

She said, "Your grandmother?"

He said, "Yes, my grandmother told me to bring this to you. She said if there was anybody in the world that both could and would help if I ever needed it that you would do it."

She said, "Um, yes, that's right." She asked him about his grandmother and how she was.

He said, "I really can't say, because I've been on the trail to you for so long.

She said, "How can that be?"

He told her it was a long story; he would tell it to her by days.

"Well," she said, "let me make you something to eat." He still would not show himself.

"You must come into my house," she said. "I must at least offer the grandson of my blood sister hospitality."

But he said, "No, my sores and my wounds are such that I wouldn't stay in your house."

So she said, "Well then, come to my mashkikiweg, the place where I dry my medicines and things. You can stay in there."

"Who comes there?" he asked. When she replied that some of the sick came and that she did her own living in that house, he said he couldn't go there. He said he had already looked around and that with her permission he would sleep in the hay in the barn. He lived in that barn for a long, long time.

When she finally observed him, she said it was the most horrible sight that she had ever seen. He used a roll of birchbark he had cut the eyes out of [for a mask], but much of what he had to say was often muffled. So she made him some new masks that he could talk through more clearly. She used some clean flour bags that she was going to make into baby outfits; she made eyeholes, a mouth hole, and ears. She told him that she had to know the details of what had happened to him. That is why she got to know the other things that had hurt him, as well as the physical problems, so she could give him a treatment that could truly heal him.

It had taken him something like four or five years to get to Onominee, and he had been getting worse all the time. Nodjimahkwe wouldn't let me see at first, though she sent me in to talk with him. When I finally did see him, it was still very bad. He had pieces of flesh that looked like they had dripped down the side of his face. His head was cone shaped. At the top were just a few wisps of hair, which looked like the wick of a candle. It was just awful.

He had been through terrible, terrible things. In one county, he had been apprehended and put in a place for the insane. He had been put in jails. So he learned to do the things that the old Indians do and like Nodjimahkwe and her family did: to travel by night so people couldn't see. He didn't trust anybody anymore, so he stole what he had to have. The worst part of it was [that] to find help from Nodjimahkwe he had to ask people if they knew her. And to do that he had to see people. He developed a technique of sneaking up on people and trying not to frighten them so they wouldn't run away. But seeing him frightened them, so he made masks for himself, and that frightened people, too.

Sometimes people would tell him the truth, and sometimes people would tell him what they thought he wanted to hear. Then he developed the idea of telling people that he was on a Spirit journey . . . and that he was not well. He didn't want to come close to them because he saw that they were kind people and he didn't want to hurt them, but he needed to find a village where there was a medicine woman called Nodjimahkwe. At last, he found somebody who knew who she was. But then he had to backtrack to bring the beaded bag because he thought she wouldn't take him if he couldn't prove who he was.

Through listening and careful questioning, Nodjimahkwe got the whole tale. I'm sure that she didn't repeat to me all of the things that had happened to him along the way, but she did repeat some of them to me, and I wasn't supposed to tell them in the village. I think I can tell it now because there are no grandchildren who've made identification with the case.

And I think it's a good example of many things: not only determination to heal and be healed but a wonderful example of a group of people banding together to heal somebody, and because they had given of their energies to heal, they cared about the person who had been healed. Therefore, somebody who had been rejected for a long period of his life was able to live somewhat normally with a group of people who were able to relate to him without being appalled.

Nodjimahkwe's treatment for the Candle-Headed Man was as much social and psychological as it was physical. She recognized that for him to be truly healed he would need a great deal of courage and support. She went around and talked with everybody in the village about the Candle-Headed Man and how important it was that they be a part of his healing. She told them whatever she thought would touch that family and get their cooperation. She didn't lie, but she thought out what would touch the wellsprings of compassion in each family.

Some of them owed her a great deal, and if they hinted at or said that they didn't want to take part in the healing I believe that she mentioned the times that she had helped them out and they hadn't given her anything.

"But now," she said, "I am asking for payment on this. I haven't really needed it, and I haven't pushed you for it. But what I gave you was given willingly, and I am asking you to give willingly to this grandson of my blood sister." In some cases, she did that, and in other cases there were people who were quick to understand what was going on. And from every one of those people she exacted a promise not to tell.

They were not to tell that she was harboring this man, you see, because he could be what some people would call an escapee from

156

the insane asylum because he had finally been paroled to work in the gardens and he [had just] walked away. I don't know how she did it because a lot of people would have felt it necessary to tell their priest or their minister. But somehow Nodjimahkwe managed to get the whole village together behind this man.

Then she told the grandson of her blood sister that he had to give the villagers an example of real bravery.

She said, "You think you have been hurt. These treatments will hurt you even more."

He said, "Oh, no, I can't take it."

She said, "What choice do you have?"

He said, "I can kill myself."

"No," she countered, "the son of my Doniita would not kill himself. You presume to take the place of Gitchi Manidu?"

She sent me out first, and I got my friends to help me. At the same time, she got the whole village looking for this one kind of puffball. Then she prepared a special poultice and gathered everyone from the village together around the Candle-Headed Man. She began the treatment by talking about bravery and what our ancestors had endured and how our people had become soft with the influx of the goods and traders. We thought that we lived in poverty compared to the white people, but it was a soft life compared to what our parents and grandparents had. We really didn't have to suffer. Our suffering was mostly brought on by ourselves.

"You want to see suffering," she said, "look on the face of suffering and on the face of bravery." And she pulled the mask off.

✳ ✳ ✳ ✳

Everybody who had not seen him before was absolutely stymied into silence. The parents grabbed the little kids and stuffed things into their mouths so they wouldn't scream. These were Indian kids who would have never done anything anyway. One woman fainted dead away, and I had to go get the stuff to rub [on] her hands.

Then she said, "You know, if this is to be, if this is the will of the Spirits, and it does look like it, the way he has finally found us"

157

(She did not say "her", she said "us"), "it's going to take everybody's energy, and all the prayers people can muster." Then she asked one of the elders there to speak to him and promise the support of the local people.

She then spoke of the role that would have to be played by her blood sister's grandson: "Now this man hasn't wanted to talk to you. Because of the affliction he has, it sounds like he is talking through a blanket, but I realize that we are expecting this kind of cooperation for this man and that he owes it to you to promise that he will try his utmost to try to do what he will need to do." He said he would.

Then she said, "I have talked with all of you about what you need to do so that the heads of families will hire him."

And that poor man. His face at that time didn't even look really very human, but he cried, over the top of those awful, long pieces of flesh, which looked like a running candle. Tears came out of his little, red, piglike eyes. And Nodjimahkwe was wise enough not to stop the flow of emotion that day. She let people do that, you see, because she realized that the sharing of emotion was cleansing.

Then she said, "We won't do a full treatment today, but it will give everybody an idea of what they're in for." She called two men, and she had them make a little rig—two logs, with a really big, thick, heavy, firm one with a crosspiece on the top that he could pull himself up on. She put him on a blanket, a really nice, beautiful blanket, signifying that this was an important occasion, and she put his hands on this post.

Then she got out the antiseptic that she had to use against the fungus and said, "I am going to pour just a little bit of it on his face, just as a first step." She was standing in back of him.

She looked around the groups significantly, and then she whispered, "This is it." Then she nodded to the drummer and he began to drum and everyone began to sing, and she poured about a teaspoon on his skin.

Because of how he was afflicted, he wasn't able to move his mouth too well, and his mouth hadn't moved before. But now it opened and he grabbed that post and it was the strangest imitation of a scream.

And all of the people began to go "Whoop, whoop, whoop." Everybody did it so if he made any noise no one would hear it. Every time he got his treatment there were twenty to thirty people around who gave him this accolade for his pain so they couldn't hear him scream. Every day she would put on more.

The tincture wasn't made out of the puffballs. I knew part of it was a little root because I helped dig it. She would inspect an area, and when she was satisfied that whatever was in there was dead in a certain spot she probed it with a needle. He never flinched with a needle. That didn't mean a thing to him, the other pain was so great. Then she would take the skin of the puffball, and she put, I think it might have been Saint-John's-wort, I'm not sure . . . she put some kind of salve on it. She wouldn't touch it herself. She must have gotten them in bulk: little flour sacks and gloves. She would take these gloves off and burn them.

People said that was wasteful, but she said no and gestured with her hands that they couldn't be touched.

When she lifted off the mask that had been put on the night before, it pulled the skin off with it. Then after a while she started saving the pieces of skin that had been on his face. She took a pair of pliers and she lifted them off and put them in a jar and passed them all around so that he could see that every time they were getting bigger and bigger and bigger. Actually he looked a lot better with the puffball skin than with his own.

Then about three or four weeks later, when he was able to wear just a little eye mask kind of thing, like a cap, one of the men came up and said to him, "We see the pain you endure, and we have never seen anything like it." And he handed him an eagle feather. The drummer played and all the people whooped and he got up with the eagle feather in his hand and he held it to us and he danced once all the way around the circle with that eagle feather.

Nodjimahkwe hadn't asked him to do that, and she hadn't told anyone how they should behave. I know that some of the kids, when he came close to their family unit, would scuttle behind their mother's skirts, but the adults just stood their ground and they didn't step away from the shadow. So when he got back and obviously had tremendous pain sitting down again, it was silent again at first. Then everybody just whooped, and they whooped for a long time.

Nodjimahkwe took that eagle feather and hung it where he could see it in the morning light when he woke up. But it was a long time before she would even let me see him. She'd let me fix his food, and she'd tell me just what to fix and how to fix it. I had to go out and whittle on some sticks so they would be flat for spoons for him.

I asked why we had to keep making new ones, and she told me, "In case there is anything that he has that anybody could get."

I said, "What do you mean, 'could get'?"

She said, "Have people been asking you?"

And I said, "Well, yes, and I have also been wondering myself."

She said, "Well, you tell those people that's to get rid of any bad spirits. We are taking the bad spirits out of him, slowly, spoonful by spoonful, and we are burning them in the fire." And that was enough for me. I made the fire really hot, and I dropped the things in it and stood back.

The village took part in the healing every day for nearly the whole summer.

Eventually, some of them came to Nodjimahkwe and said, "We thought we could do this, but we can't sustain this all the time. We need to go fishing."

She said, "You must look after your families. He wouldn't want you not to. Just leave one person behind to be the representative of your group, to speak for them."

So all the people remembered the stamina and courage of that man, and instead of it getting worse it got greater. The story of his bravery was extolled and told and parents repeated it and children repeated it and no one made fun of him or belittled him in any way.

At the same time as Nodjimahkwe was working on his face and trying to give him hair transplants, he was given a new identity. He was declared dead. They found a skeleton in a swamp near the

160

place he had escaped from. I don't know where the skeleton came from or how it got in that swamp, but I've always suspected that it was somebody from the graveyard that was transplanted. I don't know that to be true, but I bet you. I bet that was part of the plan to get him away. There was an article in the paper that said something about "God defends the innocent . . . terrible character with skeletons" . . . all that kind of stuff.

$$\text{\ding{72} \ding{72} \ding{72} \ding{72}}$$

You see, not only in my childhood but even as recently as, let's see, . . . I was at Ann Arbor for four years.

So even as recently as eight and ten years ago [approximately 1982] there was a murder, but because it was an Indian it was "Oh, well, one more Indian gone." Quite a ways back these things weren't cared about at all, but even ten years ago nobody bothered to investigate.

$$\text{\ding{72} \ding{72} \ding{72} \ding{72}}$$

The hair transplants didn't work, so Nodjimahkwe sent people all over to get black hair from the tails of horses. Then she did things like put extra slits in the corners of his eyes so that he wouldn't look like he had really big eyes. There was one place on his face where she said she thought the disease had gotten into the bone because when she removed it the bone was spongelike.

She told him, "I think I will have to take this piece of bone out."

He said, "If you take the bone out, then the cheek will fall in."

She said, "I know. I have been thinking about and praying about it. I think that if we don't take this piece of bone out that it is going to infect the rest of your body over time. If you let me put you to sleep with the puffball smoke, I think I could pull it out. I don't think it will be tremendous pain like the outside of your skin has been. It won't be any worse than what has happened already."

"But," he said, "it will make me look more pointed."

She said, "We will whittle a piece of wood for you, which you can learn to wear in there like the white men wear false teeth. It will hold the flesh up."

He asked, "Will I sound funny?"

She said, "Yes, but with practice, you can do it." And that is how he managed for the rest of his life. We used to call that piece of wood his "false teeth."

Nodjimahkwe told him that the scars were battle scars, and she said, "There used to be many people who walked among us who carried battle scars, but our young people don't get to see that kind of bravery anymore. It used to be that young people would be so respectful of battle scars, some very deep and very ugly. They would stop an old warrior and ask if they could touch his scars, thinking that some of the bravery might go to them." And she said, "You could do that for our young people."

And there was more togetherness in the village that summer than there had been in years. My father said that. I heard him say that to my mother.

My mother said, "Perhaps."

Anyhow, he lived. And he married a woman in our village whom everybody called Half Face. One side of her face had been kicked by a cow when she was a little girl, and they hadn't known what to do with it and it just stayed like that, so she was scarred and flattened on one side, [but] if you looked at the other side of her she was really pretty. Both of them had long since given up the hope of a partner. They had five children together who were perfectly normal. No reason why they shouldn't be.

"The bottom half of you works fine," Nodjimahkwe told him. "There are no scars there." But three of those children couldn't face having those people for parents, and they just disappeared.

I suspect the strong hand of Nodjimahkwe was in there because they were able to tolerate those children leaving and say, "No, we don't hear from them, but he was a dear baby" or "They gave us much sunshine." Of the two children that stayed, one was a boy who wasn't too bright. The other was a girl who by the time she might have left had a young man who was interested in her and she didn't want to leave him. So they did have the pleasure of seeing grandchildren. They were so appreciative of what they did have.

They survived just like a lot of people did at one time: they dried fish and they jerked venison and they dried apples and they got their kids to help when they were old enough. Anyhow, they're buried in the old cemetery.[3]

Birthing Customs

By the songs that were sung, people would know whether a boy or a girl had been born. Everybody in the village would know that someone was being born, and they would know who the papa was, but the gender, they wouldn't have known. The first job I ever had as an apprentice was to wash off the little newborn . . . get all the blood and vernix off its body and make it look pretty, then bring it to its mother for its first nursing. We dammed up a little stream so the sun would get the water lukewarm.

There were singers who would go around the village and sing. One song was "Thanksgiving for the Birth of a Son." It sounded like one I used to play on the organ. I played it for the Methodists once, and they never asked me to play the organ again!

[Some herbs] are used to help the baby come. One root is scored seven times and boiled gently in a good pot you could both boil and store it in. Put in enough water to cover it, boil, and then let it sit. You dig it in the fall. But you have to be careful that you really need it, because you are literally saying, "You are giving your life for this child."[4]

3. A different version of the story of the Candle-Headed Man appears in Keewaydino-quay's *Puhpohwe for The People,* which was published by Educational Studies Press, Northern Illinois University, in 1998.
4. The use of plants is never taken for granted. First, one must have a real need. Then one petitions the plant, asking its permission to be used. Only after the plant gives permission does gathering take place. If only a part of a plant is to be used, one must be careful to take only that which the plant can spare, including ensuring the means of reproduction and survival for following generations. If the root is needed, thus requiring the death of the plant, proper prayers are offered for the ultimate sacrifice of this green one. In addition, one must never take more than one can properly prepare and store.

Nodjimahkwe used another medicinal in extraordinary circumstances to make the baby come. [This was a very dangerous act because the plant is so powerful.] I never saw Nodjimahkwe perform a caesarean. I think she may have done so, but she didn't talk about it. I think maybe the baby lived but the mother died.

Bearberry is an internal antiseptic.

Nodjimahkwe said, "Every woman over forty should be drinking bearberry." She used to have women drink bearberry and willow bark tea. The willow acts as an analgesic.

Vinegar Remedy

Vinegar can help if people have an overabundance of lime in their systems and it forms bursitis crystals in the joints. You can get rid of bursitis by increasing the acid in your system. The vinegar needs to be made from fresh fruit, such as cider vinegar is. Start out with a teaspoon of vinegar in a glass of water and sip it, or put it on your salad. But be careful not to take too much or you can get an ulcer. That's what happened to me.

It's worked for many people, including myself. One time I was playing the organ and my finger just stuck in place. Another time I started to pick up a toy and I bent over and I was just stuck there. My husband didn't want me taking any "Indian stuff," so I went to a doctor.

They were going to charge a lot of money for the treatment, and I said, "It would be a lot less if you'd let me treat myself." So my husband asked how much.

"Sixty-nine cents," I said. Well, he decided I could go ahead and try. [That was the beginning of a return to my old life—or a new one—I haven't decided which.]

※ ※ ※ ※

Nodjimahkwe used to say that if a woman was worth her salt the first thing she would do in the morning was fill the lamps and trim the wicks.

She would say, "Some people hire people to keep their house or even to keep them looking pretty or to do their clothes, but if you look at a woman's lamps you can tell what her true character is."

✳ ✳ ✳ ✳

Nodjimahkwe had a log that glowed with waaswamagagod (luminescent fungi) set on either side of her doorway. She did this for two reasons. The first was so that people could find her place even on overcast nights. The second was so that perhaps those coming would have more respect for her work. As it turned out, people were more respectful, but they also were more fearful, and some were afraid that Bad Spirits were involved.

(As told to Lee Boisvert on Kitiganing Island circa 1988)

Epilogue

And then . . . I was not able to finish my apprenticeship with Nod-jimahkwe . . . at that time. It was interrupted, and when I went back there was a real difference. I had more worldly wisdom, but I didn't have the complete dedication that comes from love and cus-tom that I had before. So in a way it was good because then I under-stood better a lot of reasons for how things were. I understood more adult problems . . . and in another way it wasn't as good.

I do know that it was my greatest regret that I didn't offer more gratitude to her and that I wasn't around. I never could find the time to even worry about her often. I am so sorry for that. So the best I can do is the best I can do now.

I never had the chance, or the sense, to thank all of these grownup people. All I can do now is tell about them and hope that someone's potential will be called to the fray because of them.

To my HerbMother, Nodjimahkwe, I am obliged for many fine gifts, the greatest of which is a belief in the nobility of the human spirit. In a world fraught with the uncertainty of change, danger and sorrow, and the igno-rance of extreme prejudice, this woman managed to maintain, in splendid isolation, as truly scientific an atti-tude as if she had been university trained.

Kid Animikan, Nodjimahkwe!
Keewaydinoquay

I had seven children, two families, in my life. I had one when I was very young, too young, and I had the other when I was very old, too old, according to most people's way. I was married to an Indian, and I was married to a white man. I tried a little bit of each. . . . [of both ways of life].

In the beginning, I saw myself being the first supreme assistant to Nodjimahkwe. In the end, I saw I would never take her place. I didn't get back to these teachings until I got back to having children of my own. . . . [but that's a story for another day].

My First Summer Solstice

When I was a young girl but before my vision quest, my parents and I went to Kitiganing Island to visit family and friends. On the day of Summer Solstice, we went to the Sacred Rock, along with most of the village, to participate in the annual ceremony, which was led by the respected Elder, Bezhig-we-we-re.

The rocky point was filled with rows of people standing three deep, and canoes lined the shore in each direction for as many bays as the eye could see. Bezhig-we-we-re was there to Stand For The People, and just as in ancient times he was asking the Blessed Spirits for guidance.

(MidéOgema taught me that at Solstice what was needed was for the people to come together to pray to receive messages concerning the responsibility of The People for the year ahead.)

Bezhig-we-we-re had spent the day at the Rock and was returning, gently cradling the Sacred Pipe in both arms. He was leaning on his daughter, who supported him on one side; his son, on his other side, walked with a peculiar stooped gait, his hands outstretched underneath the pipe his father was carrying. Should the frail Elder fall, it was the pipe that had to be saved.

Suddenly Bezhig-we-we-re stopped and pulled me out of the third row. Looking down at me, he said, "This little one will one day Stand For The People at Solstice, too."

I remember his daughter tried to protest, saying, "But, Father, she's just a girl." But Bezhig-we-we-re repeated what he had said, with more firmness. (This appeared to upset my mother greatly. I myself was admiring the unusual and striking headband he wore. It really caught my eye.)

I really didn't know what he was talking about or what this meant until I returned to Kitiganing Island as an adult. I went to the Rock on the Summer Solstice, expecting that some relatives of the old ones would be there. No one came.

I went again the next year. This time I stayed for two days. And again no one came.

The third year I returned once more, prepared to camp for a week, if need be, and this time Bezhig-we-we-re's words came flooding back. I was the only human who had shown up, so I Stood For The People on Summer Solstice at the Sacred Rock, and the stones once again spoke to me.

(As told to Stanette Amy and Lee Boisvert circa 1988)

[Editor's note: The adult life of Keewaydinoquay will be presented in a forthcoming book.]